12/16/14
NF

PRAISE FOR
The Woman in the Photograph

"Mani's evocative book unfolds like a mystery. The story has a heartbeat as she uncovers the power of secrets. I found myself rooting for her, and her mother."

—Sue Bender
author of *Plain and Simple* and *Everyday Sacred*

"This is an eloquent account of a daughter's transformative journey into the heart of her mother's hidden life. It will resonate deeply with anyone who has ever wondered about a parent's untold stories."

—Elizabeth Rosner
author of *The Speed of Light* and *Blue Nude*

"Mani Feniger did such an amazing job of transporting me into her mother's world that I had to remind myself several times that this was not a novel. Thank you for sharing this important historical truth with us."

— Deborah Layton, author of *Seductive Poison*

"Mani Feniger's heartfelt account of her journey into her family's past—the moments of connection and alienation, the unexpected discoveries of family secrets—may well inspire readers to embark on investigations of their own families' historical roots and hidden stories."

—Sarah Stone, author of *The True Sources of the Nile*

"Mani's elegant writing and compelling story captivated me and took me along on her journey. It felt as though I had been invited on a pilgrimage to discover my own pre-war European family."

—Raphael Shevelev, author of *Liberating the Ghosts*

D0753072

The Woman in the Photograph

ALSO BY MANI FENIGER

Journey from Anxiety to Freedom

The Woman in the Photograph

THE SEARCH FOR MY MOTHER'S PAST

MANI FENIGER

KEYSTROKE
BOOKS

THE WOMAN IN THE PHOTOGRAPH
The Search for My Mother's Past

Copyright © 2012 by Mani Feniger
Keystroke Books · El Cerrito, California
www.manifeniger.com

Cover design by Carol Ehrlich
Layout design by Patricia Coltrin and Karin Kinsey

Quote from *Hannah Coulter* by Wendell Berry, Copyright © 2004 by Tanya Amyx Berry. Reprinted by permission of Counterpoint.

Publisher's Cataloguing-in-Publication Data

Feniger, Mani.
The woman in the photograph : the search for my mother's past /
Mani Feniger. — 1st ed.
p. : ill., maps ; cm.
ISBN 978-0-9851344-0-2
1. Feniger, Alice, 1914–1987. 2. Jewish women—Germany—20th century—
Biography. 3. Mothers and daughters—United States—20th century—
Biography. 4. Jews, German—United States—20th century—Genealogy.
5. Immigrants—United States—20th century—Biography. 6. Holocaust,
Jewish (1939–1945)—History. I. Title

DS134.42.F46 F46 2012
940.531/8/092   2012904935

Printed in the United States of America
FIRST EDITION:
June 2012

For Sarah and Brett

Contents

Prologue

The photograph of two young women seated close together on a loveseat transported me back to a lost era of my mother's life. Suspended in time, my mother and her sister gaze into each other's eyes. They seem unaware that outside their private world, the Nazi party is gathering momentum to sweep away the life they have known.

I was stunned by the image of my mother, Alice, in a white evening gown. The light from across the room illuminates the soft tiers of silk that drape across her knee, brushing her ankle just above the narrow strap of her tapered shoe. Everything about her is graceful—her carefully shaped eyebrow, the playful curl of her hair against her cheek, her painted lips just on the verge of a smile, and the sparkle of gemstones that circle her throat.

The woman in this photograph is not my mother, I thought. I recognized her proud profile; otherwise she bore little resemblance to the person I had known all my life.

The mother I knew was frugal and practical. She bought

dark, durable skirts and neutral dresses from the sale rack at Macy's and wore flat, sensible leather shoes that would last many seasons. But it was not just the elegance of her attire that startled me so. The most striking difference was that the woman I knew was never still. Her eyes constantly darted around the room, monitoring every movement or shift in tone. She was on guard, jumping at the sound of a car horn, snapping with impatience if you kept her waiting. The woman in this photograph is calm, poised, self-possessed. She is at home in the world, and in herself.

My mother never showed me this photograph, taken in Germany in the early 1930s. It was in a dusty envelope my brother found in the back of her closet. Although I had once steered as far away as I could from my mother's past, the image ignited a spark inside me, an urgency to know more about the person who had such a profound effect on my life. Long after her passing, the omissions in her story still haunt me. What happened to her? Why didn't she tell me? Who is the woman in the photograph?

PART ONE

No Wall Lasts Forever

What is not conscious,
comes to us from outside ourselves, as if by chance.

CARL JUNG

1

The Wall

As a crowd of 20,000 of his countrymen implored him to "Open the gate!" on that chaotic Thursday evening, Harald Jäger, head of passport control at the Berlin Wall's Bornholmer Strasse checkpoint, kept shouting at the guards under his command, "What shall I do? Order you to shoot?"[1]

It was the night of November 9, 1989. Earlier that evening, a reporter asked Günter Schabowski, head of the East German Socialist Unity Party, when travel restrictions to East Berlin would be lifted. In the heat of the moment, Schabowski answered: *Sofort...unverzüglich* (Immediately... without delay). Taking his words literally, and primed by months of demonstrations against the East German Communist government, waves of men and women poured into the streets of the Eastern sector and surged toward the Berlin Wall. The State Security Guards, Stasi, as they were called, were entirely unprepared for the advancing crowd. Some tried to reach their supervisors but got no clear instructions on what to do.

At 10:30 p.m., the Stasi guards abandoned their post on Bornholmerstrasse. By midnight, hundreds of thousands of German citizens from both sides of Berlin converged on the Wall. Wielding hammers, makeshift tools, or just bare hands, men and women pummeled and smashed at the hated barrier that had divided communities, families, and friends for twenty-eight years.

My husband and I sat in our Berkeley living room, mesmerized by the astonishing news. I moved closer to the TV and turned up the sound. "The Wall as we have known it since 1961 can no longer contain the German people," announced NBC news anchor Tom Brokaw, the first American journalist to report from Berlin that night. I knew we were watching a pivotal event in world history, but I had no idea that reverberations from this event six thousand miles away would find their way to my own doorstep; nor could I explain the tears trickling down my cheeks.

"Doesn't this remind you of the sixties?" Michael asked.

Yes, I felt exhilarated on behalf of the protestors. I could see myself there, the tall girl with the long hair reaching her arm up to be pulled onto the Wall. But it also reminded me of something much more troubling. *Don't you get it? Don't buy German goods,* my parents used to say. *Don't speak German in public.* The demonstrators were shouting in the language my parents used with each other in private moments. It was also the language of the Nazi commanders who drove them from their home and country.

Nothing specific had ever been said in my presence about the Holocaust, and I knew even less about the relatives that I supposed must have once existed, but the staccato rhythms of German speech evoked dread in my chest. Its harsh tones and sharp edges reminded me of a dark place in my mother, the deep chasm where her sentences fell off and the subject changed.

I remembered a remark my mother made when I was nine years old. We were walking to the A&P supermarket. I gripped her elbow to hold her back as a car whizzed by us on Hillside Avenue, a busy street near the Queens County Courthouse.

"Stop," I yelled.

"I had the right of way," she said, annoyed.

"A lot of good that will do if the car hits you, Mom."

When we reached the other side, she turned to me and said, "I kiss the ground we walk on." I looked up at her, confused, waiting for her to continue. It must have to do with Hitler, I thought, but I knew not to ask.

"C'mon, I still have a bunch of things to do today," she snapped, walking faster, and that was the last I heard of it.

∽

Every day I turned on the news to follow the events taking place in Germany. I found out that huge demonstrations had been going on for months in Berlin and Leipzig. The name Leipzig gave me chills—my mother's birthplace. Until then, Leipzig had been nothing more than a void, a place locked away behind an Iron Curtain—one Wall built by the Soviets, the other erected by my mother to obscure her past.

"What would Mom have thought of this?" I asked

Michael. But I didn't expect an answer because my mother had died of a stroke two years earlier. In the first months after her death, I felt at peace. Her stroke was swift and complete, "almost like a Zen master's sword," I told the friends at her memorial service. I was grateful she didn't linger with her capacities diminished or have to depend on other people for her care. Both would have been her worst nightmare.

But hearing the references to Leipzig on the news made me wish I could call her. I knew nothing about the city where she grew up, though I remembered an odd story she had told me after a trip to Berlin in 1959. It was the summer after she remarried her second husband, George, and he had taken her to Switzerland. It was also the first time she had traveled to Europe since the thirties, when she and her sister Erika escaped from the Nazis.

At the end of August, George returned to New York and my mother went to visit an old school girlfriend who lived in Berlin. It made no sense to me that she would want to go to Germany, or that she had a German friend. Even more bizarre, her friend said my mother was lucky to be a Jew and get out when she did. She said the Germans who were left at the end of the war suffered horribly with no food or heat, and her family almost died of starvation.

"A pretty insensitive thing to tell my mother," I said to Michael. "The Jews were lucky?"

Before leaving for Europe, Mom called the American Embassy in New York to inquire about going to Leipzig. Although it was less than a hundred miles south of Berlin, it may as well have been in another world. Leipzig was in the Soviet-controlled German Democratic Republic (GDR).

The official told Alice that entering the Eastern zone would not be wise. Since she was born there, her American passport could not protect her if the East German police decided to detain her.

My mother was not dissuaded. "I decided to take a chance," she'd said, demonstrating her defiance with a familiar gesture of protruding her jaw. The Berlin Wall had not yet been sealed and it was still possible to walk through the Brandenburg Gate to the Soviet sector. On the eastern side was a broad boulevard called Unter den Linden, where in the spring of Alice's youth the linden blossoms were sometimes so thick that when a breeze blew it looked like snow falling on the outdoor café tables and chairs. She winced at the memory of sitting opposite her sister at Café Kranzler, drinking a tall glass of hot chocolate.

She'd taken a tram to the Mitte district of Berlin and then fallen in step with several British tourists and a German couple who were walking toward the crossing. A large sign alerted her that they were leaving the western sector: *ACHTUNG! Sie verlassen jetzt West-Berlin.*

The minute she crossed over to the East, she was absorbed into a landscape of overwhelming drabness, as though all color had been sucked out of an old photograph. Security guards were posted at short intervals, and she clutched her purse with passport and camera tightly under her arm.

The badly bombed area had seen little repair since the end of the war, and most of the buildings were no more than shallow facades with a restored entrance on the street. She took a few steps toward an alley where she could peek beyond to the next street. She saw piles of debris—bricks, concrete, and twisted metal that had still not been removed after fourteen years.

She sensed the soldier even before she heard the thud of his boots on the gravel. She turned her head to meet his gaze. He was young and serious, but didn't look cruel. He wore the green military uniform of the Volkspolizei, the People's Police, and he carried an automatic rifle. A chill ran up her spine, but she forced herself to flash her friendliest middle-aged American woman's smile. She didn't say anything, preferring to be seen as an ignorant tourist, not a German Jew who should know better.

He lifted his right arm to direct her back to the main street. She nodded to signify that she would follow his command. She wished she could take a picture to show Erika what miserable rubble was left of the glamorous street where they often spent their weekends and holidays, but she didn't dare take out her camera. She turned around and walked back to West Berlin.

Watching the scenes on the news, I thought about my mother's story and wondered what it was like to see a pile of rubble instead of a street where you once strolled amidst flowering linden trees.

"I can't imagine why Mom would have wanted to step foot in that place again," I told my husband. "I never would."

2

The Family

From my birth, in 1945, we lived in Jamaica, a working-class neighborhood in the borough of Queens, New York. My immediate family occupied the downstairs flat of a two-family house owned by my father's older brother Nathan. Aunt Pearl sometimes invited me upstairs to taste her home-made marble cake or noodle *kugel,* rich with eggs and vanilla, and Uncle Nathan gave me *Nacht Süß* (night sweet), a square of dark, bittersweet chocolate, after dinner. But we didn't live there because of the sweets. My father didn't earn enough money to support our family and depended on his brother to provide a home for us.

My mother never sat still. She waxed the kitchen floor, darned socks on a scratched wooden egg, replaced zippers, hemmed pants, and replaced buttons from a jar filled with every color and shape button I could imagine; she planted tomato vines that curled up wooden stakes on a little strip of earth next to the garage; she wallpapered the kitchen with a bright pattern of vines and leaves that made it look like an outdoor patio. She also was more affectionate than my father. She often invited me to climb into her bed in the morning and told me she loved me "as only a mother can" while I showered her with hugs and kisses.

I'm sure it was my mother who chose the name Terry for me, a cute American name for a daughter who would grow up far from the ghosts of her buried past. But I was also a child who never quite fit in with the other kids at school, not just because I was a head taller than most of the other girls, but because my parents peeled the skin off apples so it landed on the plate in long corkscrews, preferred Italian opera to football games, and spoke German in low tones when they didn't want Tom or me to understand them.

My father, whom everyone called Fez (his middle name, pronounced "Fates"), was a quiet, self-contained man who always had a cigarette dangling from the corner of his mouth or a pipe held firmly between his teeth. On the rare occasions when he spoke up in an argument, even my mother held her tongue. During the World Series of 1952, when the Brooklyn Dodgers played the New York Yankees, my older brother, Tom, wanted to watch the end of the inning but my mother insisted he turn off the TV and come to the dinner table. My father turned to her and said, "Let him watch," and that was that. For Tom, that became the critical moment when Dad stood up for him.

Dad crafted many pieces of furniture for our home: a beautiful dresser for my mother with smooth, contoured dividers for her necklaces, belts, and underwear; a desk for himself with compartments for envelopes, pens, and stamps;

and a hexagonal kitchen table with a speckled green lino-leum surface that matched the floor.

Nathan and my father couldn't have been more differ-ent. Uncle Nathan was stern, serious, and bossy. Perhaps he thought providing us a place to live gave him some special entitlement to yell at Tom when he slammed the front door or to criticize my mother for "running off" to play tennis. My mother bristled when he told her what to do. She once lit up a Chesterfield, exhaled a plume of smoke in front of his face, grabbed her tennis bag, and walked out the door.

Dad said nothing. He turned his back and retreated to his woodshop in the basement. I followed him and watched. He tightened the vise on a shelf of the bookcase he was con-structing. He tenderly wrapped his fingers around the knob of the hand plane and ran it along the surface of the wood. The air filled with a fragrant, woody aroma as the curly shav-ings piled up like discarded ribbons.

୧ʃᴅ

We were the only Jewish family on the block and the Italian girls across the street frequently told me that I killed Christ. While the Navaretta sisters saw me as Jewish, I didn't feel particularly Jewish and was restless and bored with the Hebrew chanting I had to sit through when my father took Tom and me to the synagogue for the high holidays. But there was one day a year when I felt connected to my ances-tors—the holiday of Passover.

On Passover, we all participated, even my mother, who claimed to be an atheist. She and Aunt Pearl chopped ap-ples and nuts to mix with honey, a dish called *harosis* to represent the bricks of straw and mud our ancestors made when they were slaves in Egypt. They patted together sticky balls of Matzo meal and dropped them into hot chicken broth, where I watched them boil and bubble until they expanded to twice their original size. Then I helped Tom set the table in Nathan and Pearl's dining room with a carefully ironed white linen cloth and wine glasses for everyone, even me, because on this one special night I could take a few sips of the ceremonial wine. I carefully placed a polished silver goblet, brought all the way from Germany, at the head of the table so the prophet Elijah could mysteriously empty it sometime during dinner, unseen by my innocent eyes.

As the youngest child, I was trained to say the first of the four Passover questions—*Why is this night different from all other nights?* I could expect Uncle Nathan to reward me with a chocolate Easter bunny when I found the matzo cracker, called the *affikomen,* hidden between two books on the bookshelf or behind the couch cushion. Until I was eight, I still had a father who would carry me down the stairs to my bedroom at the end of the evening because I drank too much of the sweet, sticky Manischewitz wine.

The best part of Passover was the feeling of connection— that we were not just an isolated family of foreigners who were neither German nor American. For just this one evening, I had a sense of belonging to something beyond myself and the small circle of relatives sitting at our table. We were part of a tradition that started long before we existed.

At the time, I couldn't have known how much the story of the Jews' exodus from Egypt resembled the escape of my own parents from Nazi Germany. In hindsight, I wonder if, when they dipped the hardboiled eggs in salt water to represent the tears of our ancestors, they were also grieving for the people and the life they left behind.

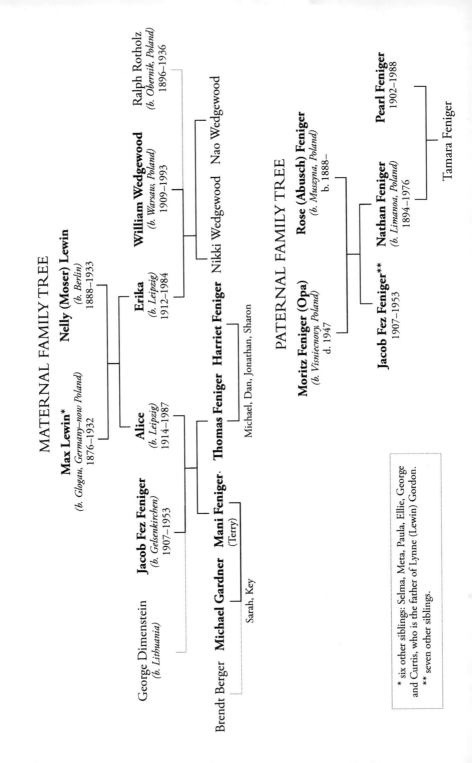

MATERNAL FAMILY TREE

Max Lewin*
(b. Glogau, Germany–now Poland)
1876–1932

Nelly (Moser) Lewin
(b. Berlin)
1888–1933

Ralph Rotholz
(b. Obernik, Poland)
1896–1936

William Wedgewood
(b. Warsaw, Poland)
1909–1993

Erika
(b. Leipzig)
1912–1984

Nikki Wedgewood   Nao Wedgewood

Harriet Feniger

Thomas Feniger

Michael, Dan, Jonathan, Sharon

Alice
(b. Leipzig)
1914–1987

Jacob Fez Feniger
(b. Gelsenkirchen)
1907–1953

Mani Feniger
(Terry)

George Dimenstein
(b. Lithuania)

Brendt Berger   **Michael Gardner**

Sarah, Key

PATERNAL FAMILY TREE

Moritz Feniger (Opa)
(b. Visniecnovy, Poland)
d. 1947

Rose (Abusch) Feniger
(b. Muszyna, Poland)
b. 1888–

Pearl Feniger
1902–1988

Nathan Feniger
(b. Limanoa, Poland)
1894–1976

Tamara Feniger

Jacob Fez Feniger**
1907–1953

* six other siblings: Selma, Meta, Paula, Ellie, George
and Curtis, who is the father of Lynne (Lewin) Gordon.

** seven other siblings.

3

Widowed

Eight years older than me, my brother Tom remembered happier days when the whole family used to pile into a 1940 black Studebaker that required a sand bag in the back to stay balanced on the road and go for picnics on Long Island or a week in the Catskill Mountains. I too had some distant memories of a young mother with sparkling black eyes who laughed as she reached her arms toward me to lift me onto the dresser and twirl my chestnut hair into ringlets, a woman with long bare legs wearing a white bathing suit, her fingers wrapped firmly around my little hand as we ran into the waves at Jones Beach. These small, contented moments came to an abrupt end with my father's death.

Just after I started third grade, my father went into the hospital. I never saw him alive again. Uncle Willy, who was married to Mom's sister Erika, told me, "He's gone on a long journey." Other than that, no one ever talked about him. I didn't know why he died or where he was buried, though a few days before he went into the hospital I had a kind of premonition of what was to come.

We were watching the *Ed Sullivan Show* on Sunday night. Mom was on the easy chair, Tom was stretched out in front of her on the floor, and Dad and I were sitting together on the couch. I leaned my head against his shoulder and he brushed my hair from my face. I slid my face against his chest, feeling the woven texture of his sweater as it rubbed my cheek. I inhaled the earthy smell of wool mixed with the slight perfume of aftershave lotion and sweet tobacco. Even though my neck got stiff, I didn't want to move, afraid I'd break the spell of our connection. The thought crossed my mind that this was the last time I would be close to him like this.

With his absence, our house felt cold and empty. Except for practical necessities, it seemed like all conversation stopped. I remember thinking, *What do I do now?* But no one answered my silent query. When I thought about my father, I got an image of his fingernails, always clean and carefully manicured, almost like a woman's. That's what I pictured distinctly, his pale long fingers.

On the first Passover after Dad's death, we didn't celebrate the holiday upstairs with Pearl and Nathan. Instead my mother bought a box of matzo and placed it on the table with a plate of sliced ham. I knew that pork was not kosher and explicitly forbidden in the Jewish religion. She served it with string beans and mashed potatoes. Tom argued with her about the ham, then we all got silent.

"It was her defiance," Tom said when we talked about it later as adults.

"But who was she defying?" I asked him. He had no answer.

Uncle Nathan let us continue to live in the house, but since my father left no savings, my mother had to go to work. She taught herself to type and was hired by a German Jewish immigrant who felt sympathy for a widow with two children to support. She practiced shorthand standing pressed against other commuters on the subway during the forty-minute ride on the E train to downtown Manhattan. She came home from work exhausted, threw her purse on the kitchen table, and went straight to the bathroom to cleanse her hands of the grime of the city and eight hours of taking orders for apple cutters and cheese graters at Wall International Trading Company. She complained of having to walk from the 23rd Street subway stop through a bad neighborhood, about the dirt in the subway, or the rude man who grabbed the only empty seat.

After putting some vegetables on the stove, my mother would unclip the rubber garters from her nylons. I marveled at how carefully she cradled the silky folds in her palms as she rolled each stocking down her leg and over her heel without causing it to run. Then she settled onto the couch and put her feet up. "A little *puschelkatzchen?*" she asked me, as I hovered around her. That was her pet word for scratching her legs like a little pussycat. I sat on the end of the couch and ran my fingers up and down her calves as she requested. I hated the feeling of brushing against the fine hairs on her legs. Mom closed her eyes and sighed. "You're the only one who understands me," she told me.

Tom, already in high school, jumped up from the table after supper, put his plate in the sink, and rushed off to the Jamaica Jewish Center where he worked in the bowling alley. "Eat and run," Mom called after him as he picked up his jacket. "All you ever do is eat and run." I wanted to defend him but didn't know how.

I knew it wasn't easy to be a widowed, single woman in the fifties, but my mother put on a brave face. She still played tennis on Saturday mornings. She followed the news and, despite having so little money, she made a contribution to Adlai Stevenson's campaign for president because he was a *mensch*. On rare occasions she went out to dinner with someone or other I didn't know, first Simon, who was Orthodox and didn't carry money on the Sabbath so Mom ended up paying the bill, and then Stephan, who wrote some book on politics but was too busy for her. I never understood how she met these people and I was never introduced to them. While she was out, I watched the slow movement of the clock and sat up in bed to stare out the window every time I heard the motor of a car coming down the street. Finally, when our 1950 Plymouth creaked up the steep driveway that wound past the bay window, I closed my eyes and went to sleep.

I knew my mother from the inside. I watched the aspirins she took from the medicine cabinet when she had a bad headache, and the vial of phenobarbitol she kept in her bedside table so she could get some sleep. She hated to be bothered by cooking, or even eating, so I had to remind her to mix two tablespoons of malt powder and a raw egg in a glass of milk because the doctor said she had to gain some weight.

One night as I was drying the dishes, I started to tell Mom about a boy in my class who spit on my desk. She looked away for a moment, then turned back, though she didn't really look at me. "If you only knew how little your problems are compared to mine," she said.

After that conversation, I invented a game called I'm-the-parent-and-you're-the-child. When my mother climbed into bed, often ahead of me, I fixed her a tray with a cup of Lipton's tea, adding just a little *schwoops* of milk. I lit the table lamp and she turned the radio to WQXR, the classical music station. "Ah, *La Boheme*," she sighed as she sipped her tea and listened to Rodolfo and Mimi singing their final farewells in a world too cruel to let lovers survive. She was no longer my mother; she had dissolved into the operatic strains of the heroine's last aria.

4

Central Park West

When I was thirteen, my mother called me into her bedroom and told me she needed to have surgery.

"Come sit down," she said, "Do you want to feel the lump in my breast?"

The lamp threw a harsh light on the fabric of her nightgown. I didn't want to feel anything, but she reached for my hand and drew it to her body. I barely touched her breast but pretended I did just to get it over with.

A few days later, Aunt Pearl took me to visit her at Roosevelt Hospital in Manhattan. We got off the subway at Columbus Circle and walked the three long blocks to Amsterdam Avenue. Mom had a tiny room to herself. The walls were an institutional green and there was a screened window that faced a brick wall.

Mom was sitting up in bed in her own bathrobe of ice-blue nylon with tiny glass buttons down the front. Her eyes had dark moons under them. Just visible beneath my mother's gown was a large bandage that covered her entire chest.

I stepped over and kissed her and then quickly moved back, afraid I might jar her or hurt her.

In 1958 people didn't talk as openly about breast cancer as they do now but my mother was very matter-of-fact about her surgery. When she came home from the hospital, she showed me the smooth, flat place on her chest with a straight line of stitches across the diagonal. She made herself a special bra with a compartment that she stuffed with soft lambs' wool and immediately embarked on her exercises, squeezing a rubber ball in her hand as she stretched her left arm further and further up the wall each day.

"Dr. Gillette says I'm his best patient," she told me with pride in her voice. "He can't believe how quickly I've gotten back my mobility. You know how stoic I am when it comes to pain," she added, reminding me of how many times I heard her say she let the dentist drill her teeth without Novocain.

Just a few months later, when I was in my sophomore year of high school, Uncle Nathan announced that he was planning to sell the house. In November, Mom told us that she was going to get married again.

"George is Russian and speaks five languages," she said. "He used to live in Tel Aviv and fought in the Israeli war for independence. He was very nice to me when I had my operation."

On Saturday, my mother took me to the city to meet George. In spite of my apprehension, I felt a surge of excitement the moment we got off the subway at 59th and Columbus Circle. The sun was shining, the trees were just turning many shades of red, brown, and gold, and the air was crisp and fresh. We walked up Central Park West, past the Mayflower Hotel where the doorman was whistling for a taxi, past stately, clean apartment buildings with uniformed doormen standing beneath deep blue or stone gray awnings. Mom turned to me and smiled; her eyes were twinkling and for a moment she looked like a young girl. I could see that she felt more at home in this neighborhood than in the drab section of Queens where I grew up.

I don't know exactly when they got married, but we moved into George's apartment just in time to watch the huge helium-filled plastic turkey and colorful floats from the Macy's Thanksgiving Day Parade pass right under our windows. It was hard to change schools, but I was excited to discover that I could walk to the Museum of Natural History or take the subway down to Greenwich Village.

Tom moved to the 92nd Street YMHA (Young Men's Hebrew Association) across the park on the East Side. I felt his absence more than I missed my father when he died. When I was younger, Tom and I watched *Flash Gordon* together before Mom got home from work. Sometimes he let me come along when he met his friends at a hamburger place on Union Turnpike. Once he and his girlfriend, who later became his wife, took me to Macy's and bought me a shirtwaist dress with pink and white stripes and little plastic buttons down the front. I understood that he had to find his own way, but my heart ached for him.

Mom and George settled into the master bedroom overlooking the park, and I got the smaller bedroom with windows on 66th Street. I made red corduroy slipcovers for my bed and had a low black table that made my room look more like a studio. I even had a private bathroom and a walk-in closet, things I had always envied in other girls' homes. When I shut my door, I imagined that I was in my own universe that had nothing to do with my mother's problems or George's awkward efforts to have a conversation with me. I sat in my canvas butterfly chair and watched *Father Knows Best* on my black-and-white TV, wishing I had a real family with a father like Robert Young. I never invited a friend over.

Many years later, digging through one of the boxes of Mom's belongings that my brother had stored, I found the copy of a letter Alice had written to Betty Ford at Bethesda Naval Medical Center in 1974. Seeking to encourage the First Lady, who had just had a mastectomy, my mother wrote: "I am, and always have been an ardent tennis player, which I still do. I do calisthenics and yoga, and this operation has never in any way given me any psychological problems." (The word "hang ups" was crossed out here.) "In fact, I got married after this episode for a second time without any anxieties. I only wish to demonstrate to you how well adjusted I am to help you and give you a lift...."

I took a breath. My mother's letter said she was so "well-adjusted." But that's not the way I remember that period. One evening when I was sixteen and in the last semester of high school, I was sitting at the dining room table typing a report on my portable Smith-Corona. George came in and told me to take the typewriter off the table and go do my homework in my own room. I felt intense resentment and shouted something about not having a home anywhere, and he couldn't tell me what to do. Then I jumped up so quickly my chair fell over. I picked up my typewriter and turned toward the hallway, but as my body twisted, something in me just blew up. I half-threw, half-dropped the typewriter into his hands. The last thing I saw as I ran out of the room was his startled look as he clutched at the typewriter so it wouldn't land on the floor.

Mom heard the commotion and followed me into my room. Even before she spoke, I screamed at her, "Why don't you do something or say something? This is my house too. This is my life too. What about me?" She sat down on the bed and began to cry. The more she wept, the angrier I became. "I'm sorry," she kept saying, "I can't help it. I don't like him either, but I can't do anything. I can't. I'm as helpless as you are. You've got to understand."

I hated how she collapsed and begged. If she had fought with me instead, I could have tolerated it. But my mother was like a fragile, frightened child and I would always have to watch how I treated her—I would never be free to be myself or to disentangle myself from her suffering. I wanted to shake her, to run through the apartment screaming, smash the chandeliers, gouge the mahogany table, and stomp on the overstuffed couch. I got hard and cold inside and felt mean and guilty. I knew then, if I hadn't already discovered it before, that my only choice was to get away as soon as I could, just as Tom had done.

5

Escape

With a scholarship from the Jewish Foundation for the Education of Girls and some money my mother tucked away for me after George began paying the bills, I left home at sixteen to go to the University of Michigan in Ann Arbor. From there I continued as a wandering, seeking, spiritual child of the sixties, hitchhiking through Europe, then coming back to New York City to teach first grade in the South Bronx. While living in a seventh floor walkup on Thompson Street in the West Village, I met the man who became my first husband, Brendt—an artist with a bushy red mustache, spectacles, and a snake ring with a diamond for an eye. He had a '52 Chevy panel truck and a loft over the bar at the corner of Broome Street and West Broadway. Now known as SoHo, in 1966 the neighborhood was an industrial area where artists hid from Fire Department officials, hoping they wouldn't be evicted for living in the buildings.

Between us, Brendt and I scraped together enough

money to pay the rent, outfit a makeshift kitchen with an electric frying pan and toaster oven, and set up a fan that blew the heat into our sleeping area through a hole in the wall. We didn't have a shower or a telephone, and the first time my mother came to visit was also the last. I felt bad that she was upset when she saw our rugged domicile but clear that I had intentionally chosen a different lifestyle for myself. We believed we were pioneers of a new consciousness, and at twenty-one the lack of comforts made me feel strong.

Four years later, when I became pregnant, we moved to the country. We bought a house in Eastport, on the Maine coast. It had been advertised in the *Village Voice* for $750. Eastport was actually a little island attached to the mainland by a causeway, and the house was only a small cabin without plumbing. The old brick foundation collapsed the day we moved in. But once again I took the hardships of life in Maine as a chance to experience the elemental realities of existence and escape the superficial values of middle class life.

Saraghenia was born on a bright, chilly, early-January morning. She didn't get the free layette the Chamber of Commerce gave to the first infant born each year (that year awarded to a Passamaquoddy Indian baby from the Pleasant Point Reservation on the edge of town). But whenever we walked down Water Street, Chief of Police Reed Mulholland would stop to say hello to the baby born after he plowed our road in the blizzard of '71.

My mother couldn't wait to meet her new granddaughter. We rented her a room in a guest house in town, but she cried anyway when she saw our tiny cabin, a déjà vu without a real bathroom or kitchen—just a "flush," as they called it if you had an indoor toilet rather than an outhouse, a kitchen sink, and a large, well-polished cast iron wood-burning stove that occupied the center of our one-room house.

Mom loved Saraghenia from the start, and I really appreciated that she literally travelled, if not to the ends of the earth, at least to the furthest point east in the United States to meet her. In hindsight, being a mother myself, I feel even more sympathetic toward her. She simply wanted to be part of our lives. The Maine winters were hard and our house was primitive, even for me, but I had to find my own way and couldn't live my life to accommodate her wishes.

I will always treasure the memory of a day toward the end of summer when Saraghenia was three. The heath across from our house, Buchman Head, was a carpet of low-growing wild berry bushes, mostly cranberries and blueberries, and the dazzling sun over Passamaquoddy Bay made the water sparkle like a brilliant blue jewel. The counter that lined the back wall of our house was laden with baskets of blueberries waiting for me to strip stray leaves, wash them, and make jam. I glanced out the window and saw my little daughter playing in the backyard wearing only a t-shirt. I watched her pluck a snow pea from the tangle of vines in our vegetable garden. She looked up and waved to me with one hand as she popped the pea pod into her smiling mouth with the other.

Unfortunately, that bright summer moment couldn't mask the growing fissures in my marriage. In the fall of 1974, Brendt moved back to Manhattan, and the following

March, Saraghenia and I took the midnight Greyhound bus to New York to see her father, and spend a few days with my mother, before we embarked on the next stage of our journey. I knew it was the right thing to do, but I couldn't ignore the irony that I had been so determined to give my daughter a happier, more stable life than I had, yet found myself a month short of thirty with a four-year-old child, a failed marriage, little money, no clear plans, and a one-way ticket to San Francisco.

6

A New Path

I sat on the bench in Golden Gate Park with a big smile on my face. The afternoon sun radiated its heat through my whole body as I watched my daughter and her new best friend chasing each other on the grass amidst peals of laughter. It hadn't been easy starting over. For the first few years we moved every six months, and Sarah, as she was called once she started first grade in San Francisco, changed schools almost as often. But we finally settled down with a housemate in a friendly Victorian on Potrero Hill, and I got a job in a graphic design firm. The most startling thing about being in the Bay Area was that everyone seemed to be interested in some form of spiritual pursuit.

One day a woman I knew from a beginners' meditation group handed me a book called *The True Sage*, a collection of talks on Hasidism, a mystical branch of Judaism about which I knew very little. Each chapter started with a teaching story from a respected rabbi, but the commentary was by an Indian guru named Bhagwan Shree Rajneesh. I had never found any comfort or guidance in the religion of my childhood, but was intrigued by the possibility of discovering spiritual wisdom that related to my Jewish heritage.

The first story, "To Walk in One's Own Light," had a quote from the Rabbi of Rizhyn: "But if a man carries his own light with him, he need not be afraid of any darkness." Rajneesh elaborated by saying, "The whole world need not be filled with light—just your own heart. A little flame and that's enough, because that will light enough of a path for you to walk."

His words riveted my attention. Sarah was spending the night with her friend, and I literally read from Saturday afternoon to Sunday night. I could barely put the book down to eat or sleep. When I was done, I sobbed and sobbed. I realized that in spite of the strength I had mustered to handle my challenges, I had lost my trust in life. I wasn't sure exactly when I started to close down—perhaps to cope with my father's death, my mother's pain, the loneliness of my teenage years, the disappointments of my marriage—whatever it was, I could no longer ignore my longing to open my heart and to find the light within me. I didn't want to become brittle like my mother.

In spiritual circles there is a saying that when the student is ready, the teacher appears. I was ready, and I soon discovered that several students of Bhagwan Rajneesh, who later was called Osho, had groups and meditations in the Berkeley area. It was in one of those groups that I met my husband Michael.

The minute I took my place in the meeting hall, I noticed a tall, slender young man in a crinkled black linen shirt with the two top buttons open. He had brown hair that reached just below his ears and a neatly trimmed beard. He trembled when he introduced himself to the group.

At the end of the day, Michael followed me to the street. He leaned his elbow on the hood of my car as I fumbled for my keys.

"Would you like to go out for something? We could just get some wine and pizza at the Jupiter down the street?" he said.

"Are you kidding?" I asked him. During the all-day workshop I had gotten in touch with my anger and done a lot of yelling and pillow beating. It was hard to imagine that any man would find me attractive.

"Don't be silly," he said smiling. "The minute I saw you, I wanted to meet you."

I accepted his invitation—the shell around my heart was beginning to melt. I knew that I had a lot more work to do, but this was a good start. Six months later, we rented a big house at the foot of the Berkeley hills with bedrooms for Sarah, who was nine by then, and Michael's son, Key, who was seven. For the first time since early childhood, I felt like I had a real family.

I'd also decided to become a spiritual disciple of Rajneesh. As part of my initiation, he gave me a new name, Anand Mani, which means diamond of bliss in Sanskrit. I wanted to tell my mother, though I was nervous about her response.

"Will you have to wear a turban?" was all she said when I called her.

"No Mom, no turban," I said.

"Okay, I can handle that.

I didn't tell her that for the next five years I would wear only red and orange, the colors of the sunrise, or that taking a new name was symbolic of giving up my prior identity. I had no idea that even with a new name, the past was still very much part of me, or that a decade later I would be as driven to know about my ancestors as I once was to forget them.

7

Safe Passage

My mother and Michael had liked each other from the start. They talked about their passion for classical music, especially Beethoven string quartets. When we took Mom for a walk in Tilden Park, he pointed out the shiny *Buprestid* beetles that lived on the pine trees or the spores on the underside of the sword ferns. Afterwards she said to me, "You better be nice to that man so he won't leave you."

"Thanks Mom," I answered. "Maybe he better be nice to me too. But you're right. He's terrific...and don't worry, he won't leave me."

Mom came to visit us in Berkeley for the last time in April 1987. The occasion was my forty-second birthday. To spend more time with her grandmother, Sarah, a junior at Berkeley High, took Monday off from school. We drove to Sausalito to see the odd assortment of houseboats on Liberty Dock.

"I like them," Mom said. "They're all so original, but

I wouldn't want to live here. Where do they put their garbage?"

After lunch we found a public trail on the edge of Mill Valley. In spite of a double hip replacement a decade earlier, my mother still loved to walk in nature.

"Ah, green," Mom kept repeating, as the four of us walked along the level dirt path that followed a stream bordered with redwood trees and bay. "I can just smell the green."

When we returned home, she wanted to lie down. I sat at the end of the bed rubbing her feet, and studied her familiar face leaning back against the pillow. In the fading glow of the afternoon sun, her normally nervous dark eyes and tightly pressed lips seemed soft, her expression more vulnerable than I remembered. I thanked her for coming for my birthday and told her I always knew she loved me, even during my twenties when I kept my distance.

"I'm really grateful," I said. "Not everyone feels as loved as I did."

"My mother never loved me," she said. "Erika was the only one.... Nobody else cared about me." I was surprised by her comment, though remembered that I had heard harsh references to her parents before: *I hated my parents. My father was cruel. My mother was weak. She didn't protect us.* I never dared ask her what she meant.

"I've learned to do some guided relaxation," I told her. "Would you like to try it?" To my amazement, she said yes.

I made a suggestion to close her eyes, if she wanted to, and observe her breathing. After a few minutes I told her to let out three long, slow breaths. "Just exhale long and slow as though you're blowing over hot soup.... Notice the muscles of your jaw relaxing...your back relaxing...your stomach relaxing...." I said in a soothing voice. I saw her fingers uncurl and her shoulders sink deeper into the pillow. I asked her to remember a happy time from her childhood.

After a few seconds, she said, "My happiest memory was going to the park with Erika. When we were both very little, we had a really nice nurse, a young blond woman who was sweeter than the others, who took us out almost every afternoon. We had a special place where we played in the grass. I can still see it clearly. I loved to lie on the earth and look up at the sky through the canopy of leaves; the sun streaming through made stripes across my arm."

I suggested that she use all her senses to relive the experience of being there again, inhaling green...thick, leafy branches...flowers and grass. As her breathing slowed even more, a small tear settled on the edge of her eyelid, and a slight smile formed on her lips.

"You are loved," I whispered to her. "You are taken care of. You are safe. You can always remember this moment and feel at peace." I tiptoed out of the room to give her a chance to rest.

❦

A month later, on June 14, 1987, my mother had a stroke.

By this time, she had divorced George and moved to a rent-controlled studio apartment on the seventeenth floor of the same building on Central Park West. My mother was thrilled to have a terrace in Manhattan, and I remembered how tenderly she watered her outdoor garden of potted tomatoes. She was on the phone with her old friend Celia one Saturday morning when she became incoherent and dropped the phone. Celia called 911 and my brother. Both the medics and Tom, who had to drive to the city from Long Island, got to Mom in less than an hour.

Just the evening before, my mother had telephoned and spoken to both Michael and me. Now the walks and the conversations were over. I got two emergency tickets to New York. Sarah insisted she had to stay home to take her finals and I had given in. I really didn't know what to expect, and I understood that she wanted to remember Grandma Alice as the independent, proud woman she loved. As the airplane labored its way east into the darkening night, I felt stranded and uneasy, stretched taut between mother and daughter. I closed my eyes and whispered, "Mom, I'm on my way."

Soon after landing at Kennedy, Michael and I settled in the back of Tom's car speeding down the Long Island Expressway.

"They had to put her on a respirator because you've got the only copy of her living will that declines life support," Tom said, twisting his neck to talk to us in the back seat. "Thank God, Mom gave her neighbor a key so the medics were able to get in even before I got there."

I didn't say anything. As we crossed the Triborough Bridge into Manhattan, I gazed out at the shimmering lights, my tired eyes blurry, the world forming and dissolving before my eyes. When I'd tried to talk to my mother about her blood pressure, she had said, "Just put me out on the ice like the Eskimos do when someone is no longer useful." One day in the doctor's office her blood pressure soared above two hundred, and her doctor wouldn't let her leave until it went down again and she promised to start taking medication.

My mother passed away just moments before we arrived. Her room at Roosevelt Hospital, the same facility where she'd had breast surgery almost thirty years earlier, was dimly lit. Uncle Willy, who was sitting in the corner, got up to meet us. The respirator had been removed and Mom was lying on a hospital bed with nothing to indicate that she had suffered any distress except for two small strips of white tape that had been placed over her closed eyelids. What struck me the most was that she looked so healthy and relaxed. Her lips were soft, almost as though she were on the verge of smiling, her forehead was smooth, unlike the worried frown I was more accustomed to, and she had a suntan.

I had assumed that in death my mother would look pale and lifeless; but she still had her normal color, a soft bronze. I thought of how she had prized her suntan, a symbol of sophistication and youthfulness to her. She made a sun reflector out of folded cardboard wrapped in aluminum foil, and on sunny days would sit on a bench in Central Park, near the Tavern on the Green, holding the shiny rectangle under her chin.

My mother's familiar graceful hands with their carefully filed nails coated in clear polish rested on top of the sheet. I brushed her skin with my fingertips and was taken aback by how heavy and inert her hand felt. Somewhere I had read that our state of consciousness during our last moments becomes part of our journey into the afterlife. I wanted to give her safe passage, as if she were a child on a train and I could pin a nametag to her blouse with her destination so the conductor would know where she needed to get off. Leaning close, I reassured her that her days of loneliness were over, that she never again had to be hurt. "You're not alone," I whispered again, and the words hung in the air.

Time passed. I heard the hum of the air conditioner in the otherwise silent room. My mother's color was beginning to fade. I felt Michael's hand on my shoulder. My brother walked over and stood next to me, and Uncle Willy glanced at his watch. The clock on the wall said eleven fifteen. We had been beside her bed for over an hour. A nurse, who had already stepped in and out of the room twice, told us she needed to attend to my mother. I didn't want to go but didn't know what else to do. I reached down and picked my purse up off the floor.

Before leaving, we all stood in a circle around Mom's bed. Something drew my attention toward the space just above the head of her bed. I had a sense of a presence, of my mother's spirit hovering there. But instead of her aging body, I saw the young woman from my earliest memory, smiling and radiant, almost luminous. Then she was gone.

PART TWO

The Search

*A safe but sometimes chilly way of recalling the past
is to force open a crammed drawer.
If you are searching for anything in particular,
you don't find it, but
something falls out at the back
that is often more interesting.*

JAMES M. BARRIE

8

The Letter

When my brother first told me that we might be heirs to a property in Leipzig, I thought of it as a curiosity, some kind of ironic joke. I had assumed that with my mother's death the last link to my family's past was severed. Even Aunt Erika was gone. She had been killed in an automobile accident in Florida three years before Mom's passing.

Then, in October 1990, on the eve of the final reunification of Germany, Uncle Willy had invited Tom and his wife Harriet over for dinner. He wanted to talk about German restitution.

"You know," he said, "many Jews whose families had owned homes or businesses in West Germany were compensated for property the Nazis stole from them. But Alice and Erika's family home was in Leipzig, and the East German government felt no obligation to settle anything. East Germany wasn't even recognized by the United States. Several times, the girls hired lawyers to pursue restitution, but to no avail."

My uncle told Tom to submit a new claim for the Leipzig property. He signed over to my brother the part that would have belonged to Erika and gave him the name of a lawyer who handled such cases. "I'd be surprised if anything ever comes of this," he said, "but you can have an adventure with history."

I didn't hear about any of this until a few months later when Tom told me he had contacted the lawyer and I would be getting something in the mail. When I saw the envelope with a return address from Max Osen, Attorney-at-Law, I tore it open and scanned down two printed pages, one in German, the other an English translation:

> The undersigned retains you to prosecute my claim or claims for confiscation of property in East Berlin or East Germany. This claim may be due to:
>
> a) Aryanization or confiscation by Nazi Germany;
>
> b) Nationalization or similar action by the Communist authorities of East Germany.

The word *Aryanization* sent chills up my spine. It belonged in a history book, not in a letter addressed to me. I wasn't even clear what it meant. The next day I went to the library. I was surprised to discover that the forced transfer of Jewish assets into "Aryan" hands started much earlier than I had ever imagined, especially in Leipzig, where a boycott of Jewish-owned stores began in 1933.

> In the end, the methodical confiscation of property took everything of value or which could be

assigned a value: houses, land, even synagogues and
Jewish cemeteries, along with books, stamp collec-
tions, jewelry and art objects of every kind, down to
the last silver spoon.[2]

I had never really thought about what things of value
my mother once had. I hadn't seen anything too impres-
sive, only a set of tiny enameled spoons, and a fluted silver
vase we kept on a shelf in the living room. Except for the
ring. My mother had a sparkling platinum ring with a row
of sapphires set between two rows of diamonds. She wore it
to somebody's bar mitzvah and for my brother's wedding,
accompanied by a matching pin that glittered against her
beige linen dress. The rest of the time, the ring and pin lived
in a safe deposit box at the bank.

"I designed this ring myself when I was sixteen," she had
told me, holding her hand up to the light. "It was a gift for
my birthday."

"Mom, it's beautiful," I said. "I can't believe you designed it."

"You'll get the ring when I die," she answered.

"Mom, stop. Why do you have to talk about that
now?"

"I'm just being realistic," she said.

She had also talked about a Swiss bank account. Her
father, a very successful dentist, had seen the threat of
Hitler's rise to power and hidden his money in a numbered
bank account in Switzerland. But he died suddenly and the
"guardian" ran off with the safe that contained his documents. Alice and Erika were never able to find the numbers
to the secret account.

"The Swiss are so honest," Mom lamented when she told me about the account. "They'll never let anyone get to that account without the numbers. That money will rot in Hell." I remembered the hurt look on her face as she shook her head.

Now I was hearing about a property, an actual home in Leipzig. In America, my mother never had her own home. It must have been salt in a wound to have to rely on her brother-in-law Nathan's charity for a roof over our heads. Did she ever dream of this property that once belonged to her family? Was that what lurked in the shadow that hung over my mother in a quiet moment when she seemed to be pondering something beyond my reach?

In the months that followed, I began to receive copies of the correspondence between the lawyer and the German court administrators. Most of the documents were faxes riddled with long incomprehensible words...*Enteignungssachen*...*Kostenerstattungsansprüche*.... They would have made me laugh if I wasn't so eager to understand them.

My mother didn't want me to learn German as a child. I was surprised when Aunt Erika bought a little volume called "German through Pictures" and offered to teach her daughter Nikki and me some practical German phrases. I pretended to be interested and mouthed the words for fork (*Gabel*) and girl (*Mädchen*), but my primary motivation was the feeling of closeness I felt sitting on the couch tucked under her arm. My mother wanted me to study French, the language she and Erika had learned at a fancy boarding school in Lausanne, Switzerland.

Now I wished I had paid more attention to the German

lessons—I was completely dependent on my Pons German-English dictionary as I sifted through the pile of papers from the restitution lawyer. Then I came to a document that put all my senses on alert. It was a Certificate of Inheritance (*Erbschein*) dated September 10, 1932.

It verified the death of Dr. Max Lewin (*Verstorben:* deceased) and identified his heirs as his widow (*Witwe*) Nelly Lewin, and their children (*Kinder*) Erika Hella Lewin born November 12, 1912, and Alice Ruth Ingeborg Lewin, my mother, born July 23, 1914.

Max and Nelly Lewin. The names tasted bitter on my tongue when I said them out loud. These people were my immediate blood relatives, yet I knew almost nothing about them—and my mother's silence convinced me that I wouldn't want to know more. Other people had photos of elders and ancestors on their mantels, but we never had such pictures. I had no ancestors, and almost no family to speak of except the two sets of aunts and uncles who had immigrated to New York.

I translated as many words as I could, hoping to find some clues that would tell me how Max died and what happened to Nelly and the girls afterward—Alice who would have been eighteen and Erika almost twenty. But all I found was impersonal legal language pertaining to the court procedure.

Nor could Mr. Osen answer any of my questions. He explained that the newly unified Germany had not yet developed laws to deal with Holocaust-era property claims that were in territory formerly part of East Germany. "In effect," he wrote, "nothing is definite until the Bundestag passes these laws." In the meantime, it was his job to obtain the documents that traced the lines of inheritance from Max and Nelly Lewin to my mother and then to Tom and me. It was up to him to prove that no one else in the last fifty years had a legitimate claim to the property.

Fifty years sounded like a long time, and I was unsettled by subsequent papers that made me realize my mother had seen more of Adolf Hitler than I previously imagined. I had always assumed that she and Erika got out early enough to be spared any of the atrocities of the Nazi regime.

"Why didn't she tell me more?" I asked Michael. "Were there other relatives I never knew? How did she get out of Germany?"

I kept repeating questions he couldn't answer.

"Isn't it weird," I said as we were making dinner together one night, "that most of the people who tore down the Berlin Wall weren't even born when the policy of Aryanization ruined my mother's life, and the people who live in her house now may not even know it was taken from her?"

"You're getting obsessed," my husband said quietly. "You know that this is a long shot and you might not get a cent. You shouldn't get your hopes up." He was pouring hot water into the filter for his evening cup of coffee, and I knew he was more tired and impatient than usual.

"That's not it," I shouted. "Listen to me. It's not just about money. I thought I didn't want to know anything about my mother's past, but I've changed my mind."

I became calmer as Michael paused and put his arm around me.

"For all I know," I said, "that house in Leipzig is the

repository of our family skeletons." I hesitated for a second. "Maybe my ancestors are calling me. They don't want to be forgotten."

9

A Vacant Lot

In November 1991, a year after unification, I received a letter from Mr. Osen, the German claims lawyer. It said: "I have gone to Leipzig to review the property and found that it is a vacant lot." A vacant lot! I wanted to find something tangible, a building with walls and doors. What could a vacant lot tell me about my mother's past? The lawyer said the entire block had been bombed in the war and the building at 32 Grassistrasse had been destroyed. Had I been naïve to think I could discover my mother's vanished life in a property that was bombed and buried behind a wall— not only a wall of cement and barbed wire but of secrets and omissions?

I needed to talk to someone who could tell me about my mother's past. Nathan and Pearl were both dead, and the obvious person was Uncle Willy, who knew not only Alice and Erika, but also my father from their student days in Germany. However, I wasn't sure if he would be willing to talk to me about "the girls."

Erika's death had been sudden and traumatic for every-one. My mother had said very little about it until she came to California three years later. On our second morning to-gether, I set a soft-boiled egg and a cup of coffee on the breakfast table in front of her and sat down. Then I asked how she was managing without Erika.

"I flew to Florida and stayed with her for three days," Mom said. "She couldn't speak, but we could talk with our eyes. The phone rang early the next morning, after I returned to New York. I didn't have to answer it because I already knew. She had come to me at four that morning to kiss me goodbye."

I put my hand out to touch Mom's arm but she got up to get the butter from the refrigerator. "What are our plans for today?" she asked.

"Three years were too long for them to be apart," I told Michael at Mom's memorial service. "I can't imagine Mom without her *Soeurchen*." That was the special name they always called each other, a combination of the French word *soeur* for sister, and the German diminutive *chen*, a term of affection.

༆

From the ages of nine to twelve, I spent every Sunday at Willy and Erika's house while my mother showed model split-level homes on Long Island to suburban "nouveau riche housewives" as she called them, whom she both disdained and envied. On the way to work, she dropped me off to play with my cousin Nikki. It was my favorite day of the week because I felt like a child, not a grown up, when I was there.

Erika designed and sewed her own clothes, usually choosing bright colors or leopard skin patterns. I loved to look at her drawings on big sheets of tracing paper, long figures of women outlined in dark ink and filled in with blue, reds, and yellows. She showed us how to cut out cardboard figures and use tracing paper to draw outfits for them. Nikki and I had long ping-pong tournaments in the basement rec room or games of croquet on the back lawn with mallets and striped wooden balls. One afternoon we were playing hearts on the screened-in back porch and Erika came out to bring us some tuna sandwiches for lunch. I asked her if she wanted me to deal her a hand. I was really joking, but to my surprise, she sat down with us and played several rounds of cards.

Willy came home from work, also in real estate, and greeted me with a big hug. His strong, solid arms made me feel safe. I rubbed my hand on his chin and asked him why it was so rough. I was embarrassed when he answered by explaining about hormones. I was really just trying to be affectionate. When I got older, I tried to impress him by quoting from books or magazine articles I had read. He gave me Paul Sartre's *Being and Nothingness* when I was twelve, though I was not as intellectual as my pretense suggested and never got past the first two pages. (The thick hardback volume was still gathering dust on my mom's bookshelf when we cleaned out her apartment.)

Years later, when I started my own fledgling consulting business, Willy sent me a check to help me get stationery and business cards printed. The typed note he included ended with, "I feel you need a booster shot for a healthy outcome and so permit me to enclose it for you. You are very precious to us and we will always be available to you in whatever direction you go." It was signed with brown ink in his sweeping script, "Affectionately, Bill & Eri," with a handwritten "P.S. the same for me," added by Erika at the bottom.

After Erika's death, I received another note on the same stationery. Its tone was very different from the uncle I had known, though he signed it, "Always Willy to you."

> *Eri's passing has left a great sense of loss in my consciousness, and the emptiness I am forced to face seems threatening and endless.*
>
> *As long as Eri was alive I had always prided myself in being perfectly able to function by myself. But I have discovered that I have deluded myself. I need the companionship of another human being in order for my life to have a purpose and direction. Being alone I face nothingness.*

In his grief, Willy lost the confidence and optimism that had made him seem so powerful. Nor did my mother's presence bring him any solace. After her death, I found a photo of Willy and Alice sitting in a canoe in a Florida swamp— both look drained and miserable. Alice, in the bow, faces the camera and attempts a weak smile. Willy, paddling from the stern, looks at nothing. His eyes, drooping at the corners, stare vacantly at the water, his mouth is also turned down, his shoulders hunch as if they have no backbone to support them. Every part of him is collapsed, seemingly dissolving into the gray brown water.

But time passed and Willy moved back to New York to stay with a woman friend he knew from Leipzig, who had "been a great comfort to him after Erika's death." We spoke on the phone every few months, and he seemed to have regained some of his former spark. When I told him I had been reminiscing about my weekends at his house, he laughed and said, "Yes, you were a delightful guest except you had one bad habit—you ate too much!"

When I found out about the property in Leipzig, I told him how disappointed I was that the house was gone, now just a vacant lot.

"It wasn't a house," he said. "It was an apartment building that your grandfather owned, with four or five stories they rented out to other people."

"Oh, I had no idea," I said. "You mean you were there?"

"Of course I was there, many times. I went there to see Erika."

I held my breath. It seemed like he was willing to talk about my aunt.

"Willy," I said, "can I ask you some questions about Germany?

"Of course, my darling," he said. "But I don't know if I'll have the answers."

"Well, mostly I was thinking of Erika and Alice? For example, how did you know my mother?"

"I became friendly with Erika during her last year in high school. Of course I knew Alice too, but she was in a lower grade, and my friendship with Erika was on a different, more intimate basis. I was invited many times to their parents' home."

"What were they like, the parents?" Here, finally, was someone who had actually known Max and Nelly.

"Your grandmother, Nelly, was timid, quiet, unassuming, almost invisible. She depended on her husband in every way. Your grandfather, Max, was dictatorial. He considered his wife incapable of making financial decisions or handling money. Erika told me that her father was a disciplinarian, a moralist of the first degree. I knew her father as a man of propriety. To the outside world, he had a very respectable appearance and reputation.

"But I remember there was a student ball, an academic ball, and of course I went with Erika. There I saw her father dancing and flirting and playing around with young girls. He didn't care how it looked. I was appalled. On another occasion, when a friend and I brought the girls home late, Max was waiting up for them. He started pulling out their hair right in front of us."

I got goose bumps on my arms. I suddenly remembered the last note my mother had sent me for Mother's Day, just a month before her death. It was a folded card with a picture of a kitten sitting on a wicker chair. She wrote:

Dear Mommy,

Today I received 2 Mothers day cards from you, which made me realize that you are my "mom" and I am your "baby." I have this wonderful feeling that you would protect me from evil and take care of me.

I am so busy lately, I have no time to moan. Never-
theless, I do wish you a well-deserved celebration in
your pretty home on this commercial holiday.

Love you, kisses,

Mom

My mother's words were so odd. At the time, I wondered
if she even realized what she had said. I had always assumed
she was referring to Hitler when she said evil, but my uncle's
words made me wonder what else had happened to her.
Before I could even digest these thoughts, Willy continued:

"Let me give you an idea of the times and how unstable
everything was. I was a senior student in the Institute of
Journalism at the University of Leipzig. I was elected student president to serve the second semester, in 1933. But
during intercession, Hitler became chancellor and the Reich announced that heads of organizations had to be Aryan.
Immediately, somebody in brown uniform stood in front of
me and told me to abdicate. Within five minutes, the new
president was in and everything was dictated by Nazis." I
could tell by the way he raised his voice that he was still
angry at the memory.

"Soon after, professors that I had known for four years
appeared in brown uniforms, the uniform of the Nazis. My
thesis sponsor, who was anti-Nazi, was murdered. When I
tried to get another sponsor to accept my dissertation, they
refused it. I realized that this was the end of my education in Germany and the life I expected. I decided to go to
Palestine." He paused.

"The reason I was able to leave so early was that your

father, who was my best friend at the university, had a nephew who was in charge of immigration to Palestine. He was able to get me papers a year sooner than I would have otherwise. By then, all our hopes and plans for the future had dissolved. I left for Palestine in late 1933. The last thing I did was to help the girls sell the furniture from their parents' home."

"The house...I mean the apartment on Grassistrasse?"

"Yes, they had no emotional attachment to the place. They packed away a few things of value. Then I left Germany, not knowing if Erika and I would ever see each other again."

I realized I had to have more than a telephone conversation with Willy. I needed to visit him in person, and maybe also Mom's cousin Lynne, who also lived in New York.

"Come in the spring, my darling," Willy said in response to my idea. "I'll be back from Florida by March and would love to see you."

The door was starting to open.

10

The Photograph

Spring was four or five months away, but just after the winter holiday season, I got an unexpected look into my mother's early life. One rainy day in January 1992, the postman rang the bell and handed me a large padded envelope. I pushed aside the pile of mail that had accumulated on the kitchen table and opened the clasp. Inside was a note from my brother. He had found some of Mom's files and pictures he had stored in his garage and thought I would want to see them.

I pulled out a plastic bag with passports and a few papers. The earliest passport had been issued to Alice Feniger in 1958, the name changed to Alice Dimenstein after she married George. It had stamps from London, the U.K., Belgium, Switzerland, France, the Netherlands, and from the police department in Berlin. That must have been from the summer she and George traveled together, and she stayed longer to go to Berlin on her own. Funny the things you notice—the careful arch of her narrow eyebrows, her hair pulled back from her face revealing a high forehead.

The second passport had stamps from France, Malaysia, Argentina, and Israel. Every time things got too tense between Mom and George—he ridiculed her opinions and embarrassed her in front of friends, or he lay on the couch all day and "did nothing constructive"—she threatened to get a divorce. He responded by taking her on a trip. She loved to see new places and meet people from other cultures. She prided herself on traveling light and thought it was a weakness of character to have to check luggage (a belief that has continued to haunt me every time I prepare for a trip).

The most recent passport, dated January 1987, six months before she died, had no stamps. In that photo, her hair is short, with some streaks of gray. She's tanned and wears an apple red Revlon lipstick smile. Her eyes looked directly at me, the way she did on our last visit. I saw the mother I knew so well and felt an ache in my chest. I wished the phone would ring and I would hear the sound of her voice at the other end.

It was several days before I took out the envelope again. I turned it upside down and dumped the contents on the table. There were several dozen photos—some more recent color prints and others in the brown tones of my mother's childhood. I scanned through the more contemporary pictures: Mom with her cousin Lynne in Paris, Alice and Erika at my cousin's wedding posing with Lynne and her sister Margie. Even in this one, taken when the sisters were in their late forties, they are mirror images of each other—Erika in an off-white sleeveless Chinese silk dress with a mandarin collar, Alice wearing a black sleeveless Chinese sheath with silver embroidery from MODES, Kowloon, Hong Kong. The photo was a poignant reminder of both impermanence and continuity. I'd brought the dress back for Sarah when we emptied Mom's apartment; she wore it to the winter ball her senior year at Berkeley High, after she had a seamstress take it in and raise the hem above her knees.

I started to examine some photos taken in Germany and realized I had seen a few of them when I used to browse through my mother's drawers as a child. I didn't take much interest at the time, except to laugh at how the sisters were posed in matching outfits: toddlers in little ruffled dresses, adolescents holding tennis rackets dressed in pleated tennis skirts and matching V-neck sweaters, even one in identical pajamas. The latter had my grandmother's name on the back written in graceful European script: *Deine Nelly* (Your Nelly). It identified Erika as twelve and Alice as ten. I had never turned it over before.

Near the bottom of the pile I noticed the edges of a photograph that was larger than the others. I pulled it out and stared at it, mesmerized by the vision of two young women leaning toward each other on a loveseat—Erika and Alice in silk evening gowns, dressed for an elegant occasion or a party I couldn't even imagine. An embossed imprint on the corner of the four-by-six sepia print said "Leipzig, Germany."

The woman in this photograph is not my mother.

The words flashed across my mind like a streak of lightning on a dark night.

The mother I knew so well had no use for frills, no

interest in glamour. She disdained people who followed fashion or fads, and claimed to not care about clothes. "It's what's on the inside that counts," she said.

After George moved out, my mother used to rummage in the garbage disposal room between her apartment and the one next door that was inhabited by two models.

"They had a party, and the next morning they put out perfectly good food, crackers and cheese and salami that had not even been opened," she told me. She hated waste and helped herself to whatever seemed usable, and occasionally she even found an article of clothing, once a running suit, and another time a sweater that she could wear.

This was not the woman in the photo.

The young woman before me never reached for second-hand clothing, nor did she eat leftover food discarded by someone else. The woman in the photograph expects her world to provide luxury and happiness. She has not given up hope. She still has dreams.

I showed the photo to my daughter, who was home for the weekend from college. I realized that when the picture was taken, Alice was probably just about the same age as Sarah.

"Oh Mom," she said, "Grandma Alice was so glamorous. What I would give for a dress like that! And look at the little cutouts on the shoes. I never got the impression that she was interested in clothes. In fact, she was always mending and adjusting her old clothes on the Singer sewing machine that you taught me to sew on."

"No, I never saw this side of her either," I agreed.

Then a fleeting image crossed my mind. "Except for one

time when I was really little. I must have been only four or five, and I think my mom and dad were going out to a party. I can see my mother standing at the top of the stairs in a strapless black dress. It was tight around her waist with a wide skirt made of several layers of sheer black gauze. It twinkled, maybe with sequins or some shiny beads, and I thought my mother was the most beautiful woman in the world, a movie star."

"I wonder what happened to that dress," Sarah said.

I wonder what happened to my mother, was all I could think. Did all this sparkle die when Daddy died? Or was that just the last straw?

"I need to find out what happened to the woman in this photograph," I said to Michael when he got home that evening.

I bought a polished wood frame and hung the photo of Alice and Erika on our bedroom wall. At the end of the day, I found myself gazing at the photo as though I hoped the two women would notice I was there and turn their heads towards me. Instead, they remained focused on each other. *Soeurchen,* Alice whispers to her sister. *Soeurchen,* Erika answers her back—two sisters with their private understanding, the world they came from still eluding me.

11

Diamonds

Lynne Gordon was my mother's first cousin. Her father, Curtis, was the youngest brother of Max Lewin. He had come to America in the early twentieth century, fallen in love with Lillian, and decided to marry her and settle in New York. Though Alice was seven years older than Lynne, they used to talk on the phone all the time, and I would sometimes hear my mother joking in a light tone I was unaccustomed to. During the holiday season Mom helped out at Lynne's Jewelry, a cozy, busy little boutique on 86th and Lexington.

In April 1992, I went to New York to talk to Lynne and my Uncle Willy. After exiting the subway at Columbus Circle so I could walk through Central Park to Lynne's home, I had a sudden impulse to head uptown on Central Park West towards Mom's building. The English plane trees along the edge of the park were already fluttering a curtain of new green leaves. When I got to the building, it looked so ordinary, sixteen stories of brown brick, a plain green awning, unadorned rectangular windows, some with air conditioners sticking out. I remembered the first time Mom had taken me to the city to meet George.

"I used to live here in the late fifties," I told the doorman at number sixty-five.

He squinted his eyes and offered a weak "Uh huh," but allowed me to enter the lobby to satisfy my curiosity. Within, it was cool, dark and empty. Familiar soft golden sconces still illuminated the ochre wall, the molding traced a bright white accent along the ceiling, and the marble floors were spotless. I glanced toward the elevator and felt a sinking in my chest. I had no one to visit.

I thanked the doorman and turned back toward 67th street, where I could cross through the park to the East Side. I passed by Tavern on the Green and the bench where Mom used to sit in the sun with her sun reflector, then headed over toward the Sheep Meadow.

By the time I got to the model boat pond near 72nd Street, my feet ached. I found an empty bench and sat down to watch an older man help his grandson guide a sailboat across the water. Then it hit me. This is what I did for the three years I lived with Mom and George. Uprooted and introspective, I was the lonely observer who watched and wondered when I would find my place in the scheme of things. I took a deep breath, grateful I had found a life of my own.

When I got to Lynne's apartment on 101st and Fifth, I was damp with sweat and dying of thirst. Lynne opened the door and grabbed both of my hands to pull me into her apartment. For a second I saw my mother—long legs, shoulders back, suntanned face surrounded by dark hair, a woman who looked "ageless," though I guessed she must be in her late sixties. She wore tailored slacks and a classic blue and white striped shirt, her carefully made up eyes framed by oversized tinted glasses. Her smile was contagious, and when you looked at her, you knew that she was not disappointed with her life.

The walls of her apartment were decorated with her own original watercolors mingled with other works. Most were unfamiliar, but I noticed a Picasso lithograph of a bowl of fruit over the dining room table. She led me over to the buffet, a rolling cart with cut glass dishes and decanters arranged on delicate lace doilies, and offered me a tall iced glass of ginger ale and some thick-sliced rye bread with several different kinds of cheese and German mustard. She had also put out bowls of fresh berries—ripe strawberries and deep purple blueberries. I felt like an honored guest, though I knew that this was Lynne's gracious style with everybody. I made myself a plate, sat down carefully, and took off my shoes. Lynne settled on a stuffed chair across from me and leaned forward, lowering her voice as if she were sharing a great secret, and told me that she still missed my mother every day.

I told Lynne that I did too, and was so glad we could talk. I mentioned that coming with Mom to her store was one of my happiest childhood memories—climbing the rickety ladder to the loft, rummaging through boxes, finding shells and beads to glue onto earring backs and pendants, and listening to the hum of voices down below.

"Mom sounded so cheerful when she was there with you," I said, "different from the person I saw at home."

I took the photo of Alice and Erika posing on the love-seat out of my bag and handed it to her. She held it in her hand for what seemed like a long time.

"I never saw this photograph before. I would guess it was taken two or three years before she left Germany. Isn't Alice elegant? Beautifully coiffed, not a hair out of place, not a wrinkle in her dress, so *soignée.*

"It reminds me of the day I went with my parents to meet her when her ship docked in New York. I was only thirteen at the time but have a vivid memory of Alice leaning over to give me a hug. She was maybe about twenty, and I thought she was the most elegant person I had ever seen, in a dark skirt and a jacket with fur trim. She had diamonds from knuckle to knuckle."

Diamonds from knuckle to knuckle! The only diamonds I had ever seen were the ones on the ring she kept at the bank.

"I came to New York so I could talk to you face-to-face about this very thing," I said. "I don't know the woman you just described."

She looked at me, the glow from the lamp reflected in her glasses. "Oh, honey," she said. "Everything's been buried for so long, but I'll help you all I can."

I took a bite of my sandwich, though my mouth was so dry it barely went down. I had so many questions on my mind, but I decided to start with the day Lynne met Alice at the pier.

"Where was Erika—and how about my father?"

"Gosh, I don't remember seeing Erika. And as for your father, well, Alice and Fez weren't married yet. Your father came to New York a year earlier." I was about to interrupt, but she assured me that Alice and Fez knew each other from Leipzig and started going out together immediately after she got here.

I was confused. "Was that the first time you met my mother, when her shipped docked?"

"No, no, I had met her before. Let's see, where to begin? As I told you on the phone, Daddy, who was Max's younger brother, settled here in New York but continued to go back to Leipzig four times a year because he was in the fur business. He kept in close touch with his siblings, and in January of 1927, he took my mother, my sister, and me with him for a family reunion. That was the first time I met my German relatives, including Alice and Erika."

I thought of the names on the inheritance document. "Wait a minute." I said. "Does that mean you met Max and Nelly in Germany?"

"I was just six at the time," Lynne said, "so I don't remember many details. I think Alice and Erika were already teenagers. They took me and Margie to a big park near their home where they met up with some boys and girls their age. I thought they were so popular and smart. I do remember the last night, when we had a big dinner in your grandparents' house."

"The house? Do you mean the apartment building on Grassistrasse?"

"Yes, it must be that one. It seemed like quite a grand place to me. Tall heavy doors and high ceilings. All my father's siblings were there, my aunts and uncles. They seemed like a mob of very big, very loud people, all speaking in

German. Let's see if I can remember their names: Selma, Meta, your grandfather Max, George, Ellie, Paula, my father Curtis, and of course their spouses."

"They were my mother's aunts and uncles? What happened to them?"

"Alice never talked about them?"

"Lynne, my mother never talked about anything from her past. Nothing. That's why I'm here."

"Somewhere I have a photograph from that dinner. I need to find it and make you a copy."

Lynne had detailed memories of the farewell dinner given by Max and Nelly in honor of the American Lewins, who were sailing for New York the next morning. The long dining room table was set for thirty people, so elegant and modern for 1927, with individual placemats, sparkling glasses, and embroidered napkins. Most of the aunts wore dark dresses that looked old-fashioned, but Nelly's was a twenties number that glittered when she walked. Lynne and her sister had spent the afternoon practicing a song their father wrote in German. It ended with "Good-bye Germany, hello America." They waved little American flags while they sang, and all the strange foreign relatives clapped their hands when the song was done.

"Can you remember anything else about Max and Nelly?" I asked.

"I really can't, though they used to send us picture postcards. I'll have to look for them. I never throw anything out! But I do remember the day that Max died as if it were yesterday. I think it was in 1932. My father loved his older brother. When Daddy heard the news, he became hysterical.

He sat on a wooden crate in our living room and could not be consoled. He mourned for days. I sat next to him for a long time but he wouldn't talk to me."

"How did Max die?"

"A massive heart attack. They said he died instantly. He was a very successful dentist and well-respected. But apparently the man was—what do they call that now—a Type-A personality? And very controlling. He never shared financial information with his wife, and he usually left her at home when he traveled. Anyway, he was on his way to give a talk at a medical convention. He was only in his fifties and he died in the taxi."

This information was entirely new to me. "I'd always assumed he and Nelly died in the Holocaust. That's why Mom didn't talk about them."

"No, honey, it was a tragic loss but it wasn't the Holocaust."

"Then what happened to Nelly?"

"What do you know about Nelly?" Lynne asked after a long pause.

"I know nothing." I said. "I had the impression that my Mom didn't love her mother, and she never said a good word about her. I didn't even know her first name until I saw the papers for the restitution case."

Lynne seemed reluctant to go on. I leaned forward and kept my gaze fixed on her face.

"Poor Nelly," she said. "I think in those days a woman alone felt destitute, and she wasn't a strong person to begin with. Max was the mainstay of the family, and from what I understand, very domineering. After he died, Nelly fell apart. A few weeks later she threw herself out of their bedroom window."

The living room that had seemed so colorful and charming when I first walked in felt claustrophobic and crowded—too much furniture, too many disparate pieces of art on the wall. I could hardly breathe.

"She jumped out the window and died?" I asked, too stunned to say much more.

"That's what I was told," Lynne said. "The terrible thing," she said, lowering her voice as though she didn't want to be overheard, "is that she didn't die right away. She was hospitalized for nine months, which was torture for the girls because she was sorry and decided she wanted to live—too late. During all that time, the girls visited her in the hospital almost every day. While they sat by her side, Hitler became chancellor of Germany, and by the time she died, everything in their world had changed."

12

The Cows

I had always suspected that something bad must have happened, but I hadn't guessed this. If I sensed that Alice felt abandoned, I had not taken it literally, until now. How could Nelly leave her two teenage daughters in the midst of such a threatening world? Lynne could not give me an answer.

"She told me what I just told you, and of course she talked about the money. They tried to get money out of Germany, every way they could."

"You mean the Swiss bank account?"

"Yes, and other assets too. You know about the cows?"

"The cows?" As eager as I was to piece together the puzzle, this was too much information to take in. "Let's go for a walk," I said to Lynne. "I can't think straight."

We walked along Fifth Avenue to 92nd Street. Lynne got us coffee at a kiosk and found a bench alongside the park where we could rest. It was a relief to sit in silence and watch the passersby—a flock of schoolgirls in blue uniforms, a dog walker with four little furry creatures on matching pink leashes, people whose lives appeared perfectly normal. My stomach ached and I barely touched my coffee, but the smell was comforting. Lynne finished hers, placed her napkin in the foam cup, and put it in the trash can.

"What's happening with the Leipzig property?" she asked.

"Not much so far," I answered. "The lawyer said it may take quite a while to gather the documents. Some of the municipal buildings were bombed during the war—he even found one paper with the edges slightly burned.

"You know, the money would be a great help, but it's really not only about the money."

"I understand," Lynne said. "Family is so important. Though believe me, if there's any money to be settled, you deserve it. Let's go back and I'll tell you what I know."

I dropped the remainder of my coffee in the trash and we went back to the apartment.

"While Erika and Alice were at Nelly's funeral," Lynne explained, "the guardian appointed to handle the estate ran off with the entire safe. That must be when he took the Swiss bank account numbers they needed to claim their inheritance.

"When the girls left Germany, in 1935, Jews could still leave if they walked away with nothing, but they couldn't take cash out of the country. Your mother told me they gave money to a boyfriend to open another account for them in Switzerland. When he returned, they asked for the bankbook and he said, 'What in the world are you talking about? What money?' Then they had an arrangement with someone else, to sew money into the interior lining of a car. They were later told the car caught fire and the money was burned."

"That's awful. Who were these 'friends?' What about all those relatives you mentioned? Didn't the adults, the aunts and uncles, step in when both parents were suddenly gone?"

"I know what you mean," Lynne agreed. "That's why the worst thing was the cows. Their Aunt Ellie and her husband arranged to take Alice and Erika's money and invest it in cows to ship to Israel, what was then Palestine. They were transforming the desert into land for settlements, planting trees and raising livestock. Anyway, that's why Erika and Alice went to Palestine before coming to America. They went there to collect their money. When they arrived, Ellie's husband told them that, unfortunately, only *his* cows had survived the trip. He told Alice and Erika, 'I'm sorry, *your cows died!*'"

We both sat there without moving. There was something both comical and macabre in the image of dead cows. I thought of how bad they would smell. I drank some ginger ale and the sick sensation in my stomach passed. I had a vague memory of a reference to sewing jewels into the lining of her dress and being afraid she would be stopped when she crossed the border from Egypt to Palestine, but I could never quite grasp the context before. It was beginning to make sense now.

"Yes," Lynne said. "I'm sure it was when they left Germany. Your mother was always the brave one."

I wanted to ask her what she meant, but my mind

drifted to another story about jewels my mother had told me on her last visit. She said that she once had thought of giving Tom a ring that had belonged to her father but Erika had it. Apparently there were a number of jewels that Erika had kept when they arrived in America. Whenever my mother asked her sister if the jewels were safe, Erika always answered, "Don't worry. I've hidden them where no one will ever find them."

My mother wasn't thinking of rings or jewels after Erika died. Sometime later, when she went to Florida to visit my uncle, she asked about the ring. Willy knew nothing about the ring or the jewels. In his despair, he had taken all of Erika's clothes to the Goodwill and soon after sold the house in Sarasota. Erika had indeed hidden the jewels where no one would ever find them. *More dead cows,* I thought.

"Can I get you anything?" I heard Lynne's voice and turned back to her.

"No thanks, I'm fine," I answered. She put her hand on my arm.

"There is something else," she said hesitantly. "In the midst of the chaos, Erika married a much older man, a doctor named Rotholz. Maybe he stepped in when no one else helped, who knows. Perhaps he offered some security in exchange for Erika's companionship. She was a lovely young woman."

I was struggling to keep up with the flood of information. It was hard to imagine Erika with anyone but Willy.

"When Alice and Erika had to give up the property in Leipzig," she explained, "they packed three trunks of their most precious possessions, all that could fit—silver, jewels, artwork, linens, furs, rugs—and shipped them to Dr. Rotholz's relatives in upstate New York, in Nyack. But things took an unexpected turn. When they finally arrived in Tel Aviv, they ran into Willy, who had been Erika's boyfriend in Leipzig. He had left Germany earlier to find refuge in Israel. Once she found Willy, Erika left her husband.

"My parents drove up to Nyack," Lynne continued, "to where Dr. Rotholz's family lived. They picked up the first trunk as soon as we got the letter from Alice, and brought it to our house in Mt. Vernon, but that was all they could fit in the car that day. Once the family heard that Erika had left Rotholz, they refused to turn over the remaining two trunks. When your mother arrived here, she took them to court but lost the case. It seems to me she didn't follow exactly what the lawyer told her to say...."

"So like Mom," I had to mutter under my breath.

"...and the man's family claimed that the items in the trunks were meant for them."

"Didn't Rotholz tell the truth?" I asked.

"I'm afraid he couldn't. Dr. Rotholz killed himself a short time earlier but that's all I know."

I could only nod my head. Max died in a taxi, his wife Nelly jumped out of the window, Erika was married before, Rotholz killed himself, the jewels were buried where no one would ever find them, and the cows died. These events had taken place long before I was born, but I felt like their residue had mysteriously entered my body and remained lodged there, like indigestible crumbs that I'd eaten off my mother's plate.

I left Lynne's apartment feeling both drained and excited.

I could feel the desperation of the two young women. Suddenly they were on their own, trying to salvage something of their family wealth to carry them forward to a new life. The two women on the love seat, once assured of the predictable course their lives would follow, were swept away by a powerful current. They couldn't imagine where it would take them.

13

The Girls

After leaving Lynne, I took the train to Syosset, on Long Island, to stay with my brother. He wanted to be included in the conversation with Uncle Willy.

It was a clear, sunny morning when he went to pick up Willy at the Long Island Railroad station. When they arrived at the house, I heard the car pull in and the engine shut off, and only a moment later Uncle Willy greeted me with a big hug and "my darling." In the eight years since Erika's death, he had regained some of his former zest. He looked handsome in a bright red crew neck sweater, a neatly clipped mustache, his silver gray hair still wavy and abundant.

Tom's wife, Harriet, offered us coffee and toasted bagels. When we were done eating, Harriet went out and the rest of us sat in the dining room and I turned on my tape recorder. I couldn't stop thinking about Nelly's suicide, and I hoped my uncle could fill in some gaps. I wondered how Erika and Alice felt about losing both parents so suddenly.

"They didn't talk about their feelings or show anything

outwardly," Willy told us. "They must have been affected, such young girls at the time. As for their father, how can two girls exposed to such brutality have any love for their father? It was impossible. He was a person to be feared. Therefore, when they got rid of him—I shouldn't say 'got rid of'— when they lost both parents and were relieved of supervision, they flew the coop. They started running around like crazy."

"What do you mean?"

"They went off to Paris and went wild."

Went wild? "Can you be more specific?"

"They were like birds who have been in a cage for a long time, when all of a sudden the door opens and they fly free. They were quite loose. They slept with different men. They shared boyfriends. They spent money recklessly. This is what the girls told me later, when we met again in Tel Aviv."

I was shocked. Going wild and sleeping with different men wasn't something your mother did. Yet it wasn't so hard to imagine the girls—youthful, sophisticated, and hungry for life. By the end of 1933, Alice would have been nineteen and Erika twenty-one, not much older than I was when I went to Europe in 1963. I hitchhiked from Florence to Paris with a girlfriend I met on the boat going over. We stood on the corner of Boulevard Raspail begging for coins because it was too late to change money that night. But my adventures didn't occur in a vacuum. I had a mother who sent me light blue airmail letters to American Express offices along the way, sometimes wiring money too, a mother who worried about my safety and looked forward to my return.

But there was no mother waiting for Alice and Erika.

The two women in the photograph had packed away their beautiful silk gowns, buried their father and mother, sold the furniture, thrown a handful of clothes into a bag, and locked the door of 32 Grassistrasse. Perhaps this was when my mother learned to travel light.

"After almost a year," Willy said, "they started to run out of money and felt lost. They returned to Leipzig to salvage whatever they could. That's when Erika married Rotholz, the doctor from Berlin. I guess it was in late 1935, because in 1936 they came to Palestine, and by that time they knew they could never go back to Germany. On their way to America, they stopped in Tel Aviv. Did Lynne tell you the story of the cows?"

"You knew about the cows?" I asked. I was still grappling with the idea of dead cows.

"Yes, of course. That was their uncle Max Hergeshausen who shipped the cows to Palestine. They had come to collect their money, and that's when I met Eri on the street. We were thrilled to find each other again and were still madly in love. Erika went back to the apartment where the girls were staying with her husband, and threw her wedding ring down on the kitchen table with a note saying 'The marriage is over. I am leaving.' You know Eri wasn't one to say anything extra. When I got back to my boarding house that evening, the landlady stopped me in the hall and said, 'The lady in the photograph on your dresser is waiting upstairs for you.'"

I got goose bumps on my arms again. I thought of an article I once read that said relationships in times of crisis and war had an intensity that made people behave differently than they would under more normal conditions. I saw "the girls" through Willy's eyes—untethered and impulsive. Forced to keep moving toward an unknown future, they became less and less attached to the relics of their past—an apartment, furniture, parents, even a husband who no longer fit into their dreams. I saw the two sisters bobbing up and down in a sea of uncertainty, grasping at cows shipped to Palestine, jewels sewed into the linings of their dresses, a passionate encounter with an old lover on the streets of a foreign land.

Through it all, Willy spoke of the sisters as though they were one person. I asked him if they used to be more alike, before my father died and Alice's life took such a tragic turn.

Willy shook his head. "The girls were different from the start. Your mother always felt cheated. Erika was considered prettier, better at school, and more popular. She was successful without trying. Alice was nervous and timid as a child. From her parents she often heard, 'Why can't you be as smart or well-liked as your sister?'"

I didn't think Erika was prettier, though maybe more easygoing and lighthearted, and I was sure my mother was very smart. I knew there had often been tension between Willy and my mother, but I was not prepared for his description of her.

"Alice counted on Erika for everything. She followed Erika around and craved the recognition and admiration that Erika got. I'm sure she desperately wanted love, but her actions did not invite people to get close to her. When she got older, Alice pretended she didn't need anyone. Especially after she was freed from parental supervision and criticism, she covered up her craving for admiration by trying to appear sophisticated, intelligent, and independent."

I recognized my mother's determination to appear self-sufficient; beyond that, it wasn't easy to hear Willy's perspective, especially his harsh, unforgiving tone. I wanted to defend her, to contradict his opinion, but I tried to remain calm. I wanted to keep the door open.

"How was your own relationship with Alice?" I asked.

"We were thrown together because Eri was always loyal to her, but we never came as close as you would expect for brother-in-law and sister-in-law. To me, she was a totally inaccessible person. I had a relationship with her because she was the sister of my wife, and she was a presence all the time because they were very close. Whether before or after I married Erika, all throughout life, these two girls were like twins."

I saw the women in the photograph, the way they looked at each other—the one reliable, unbreakable bond, even in death. When they were together, you could feel it. How many times had I walked into a room and found them sitting and talking in low tones and felt the invisible barrier. I remembered the time I overheard Willy complaining to my father, "Cluck, cluck, cluck. Those girls are like chickens. They never stop talking, and you know, if I ask Erika what they had to talk about, the answer is always *nothing*."

Willy had to compete with Alice for the person he loved most. In the end they had to share her tragic death. But instead of bringing them closer, the loss fed their resentment of each other. I could feel my cheeks burn with the heat of anger just under the surface. How could he have so little sympathy for the many difficulties that had haunted Alice's life?

I thought again of the last note my mother had sent me—*You would protect me from evil and take care of me.* It made yet more sense in the light of Willy's story. I remembered how my mother could shift from a confident, independent adult to a threatened child fighting for her life if someone criticized her or used a harsh tone. I appreciated the complex character of a sensitive woman who from an early age had to devise some form of self-protection—even if it made her seem brittle—to survive.

Willy, Tom, and I sat at the table in silence, each of us in our own reverie. I was relieved when Harriet got home and started making plans for dinner. I felt far away, caught in quicksand that was pulling me into a distant past. I went outside to the garden, hoping the sweet smell of new lawn and the late afternoon sun on my arm would help me settle down. The Japanese maple where we had buried Mom's ashes had spread out and flourished in the four years since her death. I remembered how the dry, powdery ashes mixed with fragments of bone clung to my damp palms as I scattered them under the tree, and how the air felt heavy with moisture and the fragrance of flowers. When I mentioned the lush tree over dinner, my niece Sharon said, "We point to it all the time and say, 'Tree's growing, Grandma's here.'"

I felt as though her Grandma was here—Alice looking over my shoulder and wondering why we were digging up her past. She would have hated for anyone to invade her privacy. I felt guilty and hoped she would forgive me.

My sleep that night was restless, my dreams filled with

random fragments from Willy's story. I saw the dark clouds gathering on the horizon, and the hard cobblestones several stories down below. I heard the laughter of the sisters as they turned the corner on their way home from high school, and felt the weight of Nelly's body as she pressed her hips on the windowsill and leaned out as far as she could. I woke up at two a.m., shivering.

14

Fez

The next morning, it was time to talk about my father. If I knew little about my mother's past, I knew even less about the man who had died when I was a little child. After a breakfast of bear claws and coffee, I asked Willy how well he had known my father.

"I knew your father from the university in Leipzig. We were in the fencing club. I don't think there was ever a man who was a better friend to me, or—I hope—I to him. We were very close. Often he would stay over and we talked half the night. Fez was a highly intelligent, sensitive man, and I don't think he would hurt a fly, but it was another story with his father."

He turned to my brother. "You knew him, didn't you Tom?"

"Yes, I knew Opa," Tom said. "He only spoke German, and we all took turns going upstairs to visit him for a half hour each day. That's how I learned a little German."

"I only know him from a few photos of a tall, gaunt man with a little two-year-old me in a snowsuit," I added.

Willy continued, "During our school vacation, your father took me to meet his family near Essen. I don't remember his mother; she must have already passed away. But his father left quite an impression on me. Old man Feniger was stern and imperious, a religious fundamentalist. I was excited about my newly acquired knowledge, and I spoke to him about the sun being the source of energy and the moon being a dead planet. He jumped out of his chair and started yelling at me: 'It is written that God created the sun to shine by day and the moon to shine by night. Get out of my house!'

"And here was Fez, the youngest of nine siblings, who loved the good life. Oh my god, how the girls adored him. When we were at the university, we used to go quite often to Berlin, where certain restaurants had tables with pipes that could transport mail. Each table had a pad of paper and a tube so you could direct your message to other tables.

"You should have seen your father!" Here Willy made a flourish with his hand, "The poems and notes he got! I remember a note that read, 'To the man with the sad eyes, I'd love to meet you.'"

I tried to picture my father's face. Were his eyes sad? He had been gone so long that I hardly remembered him, but for a split second I had an image of his wistful gray-green eyes and clean shaven face bearing an enigmatic half-smile that captivated the attention of the well-dressed young women at the next table. He lifted his glass of wine to his lips as he turned to look in their direction.

"So how did he and Alice meet each other?" I asked.

"Initially, through me. Your father and I were part of

a larger social group of young men and women. We did things together—hikes in the mountains, trips to the seashore, picnics, parties. Alice was only one of the girls Fez went out with. But I can tell you, she wanted him from the start."

"So what happened?" I asked. "With all the moving around, how did they find each other again?"

"I always assumed they got married in Germany," said Tom.

"No, no. Your father came to New York at least a year earlier than the rest of us. When he left Germany he was in love with another girl, Annalie was her name. She didn't get out until much later. When Fez came here, he was alone, completely uprooted from his family and his society. When I arrived, he naturally found himself spending time together with Erika and me and your mother. Alice was convenient, someone familiar from the life he left behind."

I had a feeling in my chest like a rock had lodged there. Willy looked down at his pad of paper.

"What is it?" I asked.

"A note I scribbled that I find very symptomatic and important. I wrote, 'Your mother was attracted to men who were successful and strong, but her tragedy was that she picked weak ones. Your father was weak in character.'"

Tom leaned forward at the table. "What you mean weak in character?" he asked.

"For instance, he was weak enough to get involved with a woman…whom he didn't want to marry."

"Do you mean he didn't want to marry Alice?" I asked, struggling to keep my voice neutral.

"Fez didn't have any ambition to have a family or earn a living. In Leipzig, his older brother Nathan took care of him. Nathan ran the fur business in Leipzig and Fez went in every Friday to collect his paycheck. In New York, he tried to start his own fur business. He used some of the money your mother brought—I assume about $15,000, same as Eri—a sizable amount in the 1930s but not enough to live on. He made himself a nice office with a big desk and plush carpets, but he had no idea how to run a business. He had problems with the union, and they pressured him to hire certain workers and everything went wrong. This gentle, sensitive person was thrown into a world where the requirement for survival was toughness, and he didn't have it."

"But I remember Daddy coming home and his hands would be black because he was cutting pelts," Tom said.

"Yeah, maybe one or two of them," Willy said with a shrug of his shoulders.

"You know, if he could have stayed in Germany, maybe your father would have finished law school. With his intelligence and articulate language, he might have been a very persuasive attorney. Or he could have continued to be supported by his brother in the fur business and lived as the thoughtful, gentle person he was. But here he was in a new situation. He never quite found his place. He couldn't cope with the pressures and responsibilities of a wife and family. At the end of his life, he felt like a failure. Your father always had one foot in this world and one in the next. I have the feeling your father didn't die of heart failure. He died of a broken heart."

I wished I didn't know what Willy meant, but as he

spoke, I sensed the poetic sensibility of a man who read good literature, carved fine furniture, but who lacked my mother's determination and resilience, the traits that helped her go on.

I thought of Lynne's comment that Alice was not bitter in the beginning, and of the photos of Alice and Fez in an album my mother made in 1936, soon after she arrived in New York. My favorite picture of my parents shows my father, a handsome young man with wavy hair, an open white shirt, and trousers rolled up to his knees, reaching out his arm to steady my mother on a rock outcrop over the waves at Coney Island. Her skirt is blown up by the wind, exposing her shapely leg and thigh as she grasps his arm. My uncle's words could not erase the picture of my parents that I saw with my own eyes.

But Willy repeated that Fez didn't want to marry my mother.

"Then why did he?" I asked, getting increasingly irritated at the insistence in my uncle's voice.

"Your father came to me for advice. He didn't know what to do. He had been going out with Alice since she arrived in New York, but he was still in love with the other girl."

"Annalie?"

"Yes. He had no idea when or if Annalie would come here. All night long we talked. Your father paced back and forth until dawn. But he had to face the reality, and by morning he had made a decision. You see, Alice was pregnant."

The day had started off so sunny and cheerful. I looked out the sliding glass doors and saw that clouds were gathering on the horizon. I felt too bruised to speak. It was not just the information, but Willy's indifference towards my mother, his pity for my father.

"You know," my uncle said after a long silence, "when we think of the Holocaust, we think of the six million people who were killed in the concentration camps. Actually there are many more people who are victims. Your mother and father, Erika and I, are also victims, because everything that has happened in our lives is a result of being so completely uprooted."

15

Tangled Web

After Willy left, I sat down in the den with Tom and Harriet. Even though it was a warm evening I felt chilled, my spirits dampened by our conversation. I pulled a knitted throw over my legs and was grateful for the hot mug of tea that Harriet handed me. It was not that I had assumed that everything was rosy and romantic, Ingrid Bergman and Humphrey Bogart having a passionate love affair while escaping from the Nazis in Casablanca, but I did expect to hear of a happy time when my mother and father were young and in love. I felt as though a private treasure I had hidden away for safekeeping had been exposed and damaged. I asked Tom how he felt.

"I don't really have a strong reaction. I saw Mom as a very manipulative person and it didn't surprise me that she was pregnant. The agonizing part for me was imagining what Bill and Dad said to each other that night. Bill made it sound like he was the one who convinced Fez to do the right thing."

"Yeah, he made it sound that way, but we don't know what was really going on. You don't get pregnant alone."

"No, of course you don't. I see your point. I admit, I've always felt more sympathetic to Dad than Mom." Tom paused for a moment. "But here's this man who was the hit of Leipzig, good looking, charming. Every woman wanted him. Alice marries him, and he isn't the husband she imagined. It really is another great disappointment for her. I can see how she must have felt cheated once again."

I felt my eyes well up when I heard Tom express some sympathy for our mother. I knew that he didn't have an easy relationship with her. No matter how hard he tried, he could never make up for the husband who had let her down.

"However it came about," Tom said, "if you had asked me, I would have told you that Mom and Dad had a reasonably happy marriage in the beginning, at least when I was young. I have a memory of Dad swinging her around in the kitchen, and I remember them talking and laughing, or having Bill and Erika over to play bridge. And in the summer Dad drove us to Jones Beach, of course, with the two of them in the front seat smoking the whole time. I can see some truth in what Bill said, but I don't see it as all true, not the whole story."

I agreed and, for the moment, chose to leave the subject at that. I was afraid that churning up the past would erode the closeness I craved with both my brother and my uncle.

Before I got ready for bed, I called Lynne to apologize for not being able to come over once more before I left New York.

"That's too bad," she said. "Don't let too much time pass until you visit again...and bring that beautiful daughter of yours next time."

"I promise."

I heard a plane in the distance, probably on its way to JFK, and the hum of the dishwasher in the kitchen.

"Lynne, just one more thing. Did you know...." I hated to say it but I really had to ask. "Did you know about Mom being pregnant?"

"Yes," she answered after a pause. Her voice dropped so low that I had to strain to hear her. "I remember the night your father came to our house in Mt. Vernon to ask my parents for advice. He sat in our living room for hours, talking and smoking one cigarette after another until the wee hours of the morning. You know, Alice was crazy about your father."

"I know."

Just before we said good-bye, Lynne said quietly, "Your mother lost so much, she could never look back." I thought of the photos from Coney Island, the image of my parents' exhilaration, fluid and alive as the waves crashing at their feet. I wished a person could store happiness the way a photo freezes a perfect moment.

The plane ride home was turbulent, but it wasn't the air. I tried to get comfortable in my seat, to watch the movie, to read the in-flight magazine. But no matter where I looked I saw Alice—a sensitive young girl who follows her older sister to the park to play with her friends, who tries to act with bravado but tiptoes across the dining room at home hoping her father will not criticize her that day, a high school girl who falls in love with a sensitive college student but knows she can't hold on to him. Then in the turbulence of history, she finds him again on a cliff overlooking the sea, and they fall into each others' arms to remain forever.

But that isn't what happened. A few days later Tom called to say he found their marriage certificate. "Their marriage certificate says February 24, 1937. I was born six months later."

"I guess that's it then," I said. "They never celebrated a wedding anniversary, did they?"

"No, and I never really thought about it."

The following week, Willy called. He said I should talk to Annalie—the woman my father supposedly left behind. I was stunned. I wavered, feeling both nervous and curious. But I was determined to make some sense out of the tangled past, and Annalie was a thread I couldn't dismiss whether I liked the emerging picture or not.

"She's married, of course, and lives in New Jersey. Here's her phone number," he said.

My heart throbbed as I dialed her number. When she picked up the phone, I explained that my uncle had given me her number and I was the daughter of Alice and Fez Feniger. After a brief pause, she said, "Yes, hello," in a German accent much stronger than my mother's.

"My uncle told me that you were close to my father in Leipzig and might be able to tell me about him."

"I won't talk about your father," she said emphatically.

Her abruptness shocked me for a minute; then I found my voice.

"You don't have to say anything private. Just tell me about him as a person. He died when I was so young. I didn't really get to know him."

"I have nothing to say," she repeated.

Then she told me that she knew Alice and Erika from their school days, though she was closer to Erika. "Their father was my dentist, and I was always afraid of him. I went to their house for birthday parties. The other children didn't like to go to parties at their house because their father acted so peculiar."

"In what way?" I asked.

"I have nothing more to say. I won't talk about those who are not here to defend themselves. Good-bye."

She hung up. That was it. I was left speechless, empty, a knot in my chest.

When I told my uncle that I was disappointed, he said, "I didn't think she would talk to you."

"There are too many secrets," I told Michael that evening, "too many omissions, way too much held back. I hate it. You used to hide things from me," I continued, balanced on a narrow ledge between grief and anger. "I couldn't stand it if you did that now."

"I don't do that now. That's why we've worked so hard to face difficult things. I'm not holding back anything. I promise. Come here."

I walked over to him and sat on his lap, but before I could let him comfort me, I needed to tell him something I never told anyone, not my mother or Willy or Tom.

"I hardly have any memories of my father. He died

so long ago, and any reminder of him was so completely erased. But there is one moment I still recall in vivid detail, as though it was carved into my brain.

Michael lifted my face so he could look into my eyes.

"I was sent to Willy and Erika's house the weekend after he died. A few nights after I returned home, something startled me awake in the middle of the night. I sat straight up in bed, my eyes wide open and alert. That's when I saw him, my father, walk right through the door that led from my parents' bedroom into mine. He looked just as I knew him, in loose trousers and shirtsleeves rolled up, but he was greenish and transparent. He took a step in my direction. I got scared and closed my eyes. When I opened them, he was gone. I didn't say a word to anyone, because we never talked about him again. But I've always been angry at myself because I made him go away. I missed my chance to say good-bye to him. Maybe he was coming to tell me he loved me, and now I'll never know."

16

Juden Verboten

Ich erkläre hiermit mein Einverständnis damit das
meiner Ehefrau Erika Hella Rotholz, geborne Lewin,
bevollmächtigt ist, das Grundstück Grassistraße 32
zu verkaufen.

I declare herewith my consent that my wife
Erika Hella Rotholz, born Lewin, is authorized by
me to sell the property at 32 Grassistrasse.

The statement was signed by Dr. Ralph Rotholz on
November 19, 1935, part of the growing file of documents
with their official seals of the *Amtsgericht Leipzig* (Leipzig
District Court), that provided more evidence of the vanished past I sought to recover. Before, Dr. Rotholz was just
a minor character in Erika and Willy's story. But the court
records revealed his true importance. As Erika's husband, his
permission had been required to sell the Leipzig property.

The doctor's name in print also made it impossible for

me to ignore the disturbing image of a liaison between a displaced young woman and a much older man who later took his own life. Years after, I learned that Erika had told her children that her first husband jumped off the Empire State Building. I don't know what surprised me more, the man's bizarre death or that Erika had actually told her children about it. She also told them that she once bumped into Hitler on the street—*literally bumped into him*. She wasn't paying attention to where she was running. He told his henchmen to leave the young woman alone.

The *Erbschein*, the Certificate of Inheritance, of Nelly's death on June 12, 1933, naming Alice and Erika as her beneficiaries, confirmed the story of my grandmother's rash decision. I counted the months on my fingers: October, November, December, to June 12th, exactly nine months, almost to the day, from Max's death. Her final act, which left her two teenage daughters alone in an unpredictable world, went beyond simply a failure to protect. Of course my mother didn't want me to know.

Nelly's choice haunted me like a disturbing movie that played over and over in my mind. I imagined her life in the days after Max's death. She was unable to think clearly or attend to the simplest household matters, unable to eat. She must have stayed in her bedroom, and when the girls went in to talk to her, she alternated between silent depression and near hysteria. Nelly's life was in turmoil, the country was in chaos, and she believed she was destitute. Absorbed in her own dilemma, she would hardly have noticed that her daughters were confused and didn't know what they should do.

I sat at my kitchen table and gazed out past our deck as the sun sank under the Golden Gate, leaving me in shadows. I was overcome by a sharp pain in my belly, an urge to cry, then a numb sensation, an impression of emptiness in my chest. I had a perception I recalled from childhood, that I was experiencing my mother's suppressed feelings. It seemed to me that there were things my body knew without her telling me.

My inner turmoil was too great to manage alone. I called a friend.

"Your grandmother committed suicide?" she said. "That's awful. I'm so sorry."

The explicit word, *suicide,* made me recoil. I wasn't ready to hear it or say it. I had a gnawing memory of my mother's sarcastic references to death—"put me out on the ice"—and I wondered how much Nelly's action had colored Mom's thoughts.

My friend brought me a book about Charlotte Salomon, a German Jewish artist, born in Berlin in 1917, who was the daughter of a prominent surgeon. Salomon's mother jumped from a four-story window when she was a child of nine; her father originally told her the cause of death was influenza, but thirteen years later, when her grandmother made an unsuccessful suicide attempt, she learned the truth. Throughout Charlotte's short life, until she was killed in Auschwitz in 1943, she used art to make sense of her life. She drew a picture of her mother filling a window frame, then a second drawing with only the empty frame. The author wrote, "The recovery of a silenced past became her project, her protection."[3]

I learned that suicide, *Selbstmord,* was widespread among the middle- and upper-class German Jewish women of that period. Though educated and cultured, they often found themselves trapped in a situation that gave them no power over their lives and no opportunity to express their intelligence. Salomon's biographer, Mary Lowenthal Felstiner, was considered a pioneer for writing about the devastating effects of sexism instead of minimizing its impact under the larger shadow of the Holocaust. Though I had hardened my heart toward Nelly on my mother's behalf, the book gave me a new context and a glimmer of compassion for my grandmother's despair.

More documents surfaced, with more dates and details. When Tom had searched his basement to find our parents' marriage license, he came across other papers. Among them was a *Carte d'Identité,* an identity card issued to Alice Lewin, age nineteen, in Paris, dated December 1933. Alice's face is young, open, with soft sparkling eyes and a cheerful smile. She is wearing a jacket with a black Persian lamb collar, her scarf tucked in and secured by a pin. In her international driver's license, issued in Berlin just one year later, 1934, *Angaben über den Führer* (under the Führer), her face is that of a serious adult, with worried eyes, a drawn expression, older than her years.

I explored the history of Germany from 1933 to the end of 1935. As my uncle had indicated, everything started to change immediately after Hitler became Reich Chancellor on January 30, 1933. In March of that year, the Enabling Act gave him unlimited powers and the Reichstag became a mere rubber stamp for Nazi edicts. In April, the

Nazi party proclaimed a general boycott of Jewish-owned businesses and passed laws to dismiss non-Aryan civil service employees and to deny Jewish attorneys admission to the bar. Propaganda Minister Joseph Goebbels called for rallies and book burnings to protect German minds from being "tainted" by foreign and Jewish authors. In May, over twenty thousand books were thrown into a bonfire at Opernplatz (Opera Square), in Berlin. *Juden Verboten* (Jews Forbidden)—signs were displayed in public facilities, businesses, stores, and restaurants.

Willy said that the excitement of living in Paris had worn thin, along with their reserve of cash, so Alice and Erika returned to Leipzig. They found circumstances were worse than when they left. Perhaps it was at this point that Rotholz entered the picture. Did he mean to offer strength and protection to Erika, or did he seize the opportunity to take advantage of a very attractive but lost young woman?

I could see them staring at the *Juden Verboten* sign in the window of a café they once frequented, while further down the street they were denied entrance to the dressmaker's shop. They would have felt the absence of many of their friends, including Fez and Willy. Others, whose families owned businesses and properties, were trying to stay where they were until the German people came to their senses and got rid of the crazy Führer. Many were convinced that the Germans were rational and would return to the rule of law. They decided to wait out the shocking changes rather than flee, leaving everything they had worked so hard for behind. For the girls, there was no question. There was nothing left to hold them. Perhaps that was their good fortune after all.

17

A Broken Thread

In June 1992, we were notified that a real estate development company called Neue Leipziger had signed a provisional contract for the purchase of the Leipzig property. The fulfillment of that agreement was still conditional on our being able to prove that we were the rightful heirs. A month later I received a bound orange folder, twenty pages of German legal language with an official notarized seal, the *Beglaubigte Abschrift* (certified copy) from the notary in Berlin. The cover letter from the lawyer explained: "The situation remains unsettled but positive." He also sent a chronological summary of the Leipzig property, just dates and property transfers, but as I read it, the human history rose up before me like a phoenix from the ashes.

Dr. Max Lewin bought the building at 32 Grassestrasse on March 20, 1920. His dentistry office was doing well, and he wanted to provide his family with a home in the prestigious Music Quarter. When Erika and Alice were little, the spacious apartment with its tall ceilings and heavy doors seemed enormous. As they got older, it became darker and more confining. The heavy Persian rugs on the floor and gloomy oil paintings on the walls offered little comfort when Max was in a volatile mood.

But Alice loved being outdoors in the green ocean of Leipzig's parks, or running down the street on her way to school, the smack of her feet on the cobblestone streets and her shouts to Erika creating echoes that bounced from building to building. She dreaded the moment at the end of the day when they returned home and opened the front door, hoping her father would not be sitting in the dining room with a frown.

This was also the apartment where as teenagers the girls dressed in their beautiful gowns for special occasions, where they brushed their hair and each helped the other with the clasp on a necklace or bracelet. It was here that Alice ran her hands over the soft ruffles of her evening dress as she prepared for a dinner that would take place after opening night of the Gewandhaus Orchestra.

In October 1932, Max died of a heart attack. By January, Nelly lay critically injured in the hospital, and Hitler was Chancellor of Germany. Their privileged life, built on the solid stone of 32 Grassistrasse, had begun to crumble. On December 10, 1935, Alice and Erika were forced by the policy of Aryanization to sell the property at below its value to an Aryan buyer, Dr. Walther Brauer. At the time of the sale, Erika was married, and her husband, Dr. Ralph Rotholz, consented to the sale as required by German law.

Immediately after the transaction was completed, Alice, Erika, and Ralph Rotholz fled to Palestine. The ruffled gowns, the sparkling necklaces and the memories were left behind, except for three trunks shipped to Nyack, New York.

During World War II, the building was destroyed by bombing: *Grundstück wurde im Krieg zerstört.* On May 9, 1969, while Leipzig was under the domination of the Communist German Democratic Republic, Dr. Bauer sold the empty lot to the city of Leipzig. Nothing was ever built on it. In 1990, Tom and I presented our case as the legitimate heirs to the property, and in a sense, to its history.

The next time I called Uncle Willy, I told him about the signing of the provisional contract. Since our meeting two months earlier, I had spoken to him on the phone several times, though not about the past. The conversations about my parents threatened to take away the fleeting positive impressions I had of their marriage, and—perhaps even more painful to me—exposed a judgmental side of Willy I didn't want to focus on. The affection between us was a safe, cherished part of my childhood. For my own sake, I chose to be loyal, not just to Willy, but to the warmth and longevity of our relationship.

Willy was stunned to hear about the contract. "You're kidding!" he said several times, and he repeated that he had not expected anything to come of it. I told him it still wasn't a sure thing. "Isn't it amazing that something lost so long ago could be found again?" I marveled. He said he was happy, but I heard him clear his throat and pause before he spoke. I had a sense that the news confused and troubled him, though I didn't press further.

In September, my brother called to tell me that my uncle was in Mt. Sinai hospital in New York. The doctors didn't know what was wrong, but he had stopped eating and was slipping in and out of consciousness. The news hit me hard. I was not willing to lose him without a farewell. I booked a flight to New York the next day.

I took a taxi from the airport and went straight to the hospital. My uncle's eyes were closed, but he opened them wide and said, "What are you doing here?" then dozed off again. During the two hours I stayed, he awakened again and we had a brief, tender conversation. The next day the nurse told me there was no medical diagnosis that required hospital treatment and he would go to a nursing home on Long Island to spend his last months near his daughters, both of whom were married and lived in the area. I offered to ride with him in the ambulance.

Sitting on a bench in the back of the ambulance, my nerves felt prickly. It was hard to see my robust, assertive uncle so fragile, clothed in a hospital gown, strapped into a bed. I often got anxious riding in the back seat of a car and I had a surge of panic at the thought of the ambulance charging down the freeway, siren blaring to force other vehicles out of our path. To assuage my anxiety I started a conversation with the attendant sitting next to me. He assured me that this was not an emergency and they would drive at a normal speed without sirens. I continued to ask him questions, more to calm myself with the distraction than out of genuine curiosity.

Suddenly Uncle Willy opened his eyes, turned his head toward me and said in a loud, irritated voice, "Can you please stop talking? Can't a man get some rest?" He drifted right back to sleep but I felt the sting of his reprimand, like a child who had lost parental favor.

I stayed a few days and visited him once he was settled in the nursing home. The time was precious to me because I was able to say good-bye in loving words I hadn't had the chance to express to Dad, Mom, or Erika. A month after I left, Tom called to let me know that Uncle Willy was on the mend. A friendly Irish nurse had told him that if he was trying to find a way to die, not eating would take a very long time and it probably wasn't the best method. Apparently she was persuasive because he started to eat again and was released a month later. When he moved back to Sarasota I called him in his new residence at a hotel overlooking the beach.

"What happened?" I asked. "How did you get better?"

"Food and friends," he answered. "That's what brought me back. Food and friends."

In January 1993 I received a letter from my uncle. "My life here is rather quiet and each day follows the other without excitement and without interest in the world's daily rush," he wrote. Two months later, March 19, 1993, he passed away.

My Uncle Willy was the last to die among the adults I loved and considered my elders. I rarely saw Uncle Nathan after we moved out of the house in Queens, though I had visited him one last time when he was in his eighties. I went by the apartment on West End Avenue in Manhattan where he and Aunt Pearl lived, a small, neatly furnished two-bedroom with walls lined with books. He didn't have much to say, but when he took my hand, his eyes brimmed with tears, and I saw the tender, affectionate side of him, finally available once all the responsibilities of his adult years were behind him. He died soon after, and Aunt Pearl was moved to a nursing home. There was an entry in my mother's date book on the day she died: "Visit Pearl at 4 p.m." I wondered if anyone called Pearl to tell her that Alice wasn't coming.

Nathan and Pearl, Alice and Fez, Erika, and now Willy. I was grateful to Willy for breaking the long silence about the past. He was a living witness who provided a thread, albeit a tangled one, to connect me to my parents. With his death, the thread was broken, and I felt as though I lost all of them for good.

18

The Dinner Party

The photo of Alice and Erika hung on my bedroom wall, calling to me from their private world. I continued to imagine scenes from their lives, but I didn't know how to proceed in my quest. The only person who actually liked to talk about family was Lynne. I was no longer the little girl who climbed into the loft of her jewelry store to string beads. Even though she was twenty-four years older than me, we turned to each other to fill the void left by my mother's death. Lynne wrote me notes in her flowing script with a flourish on the capital letters:

> *I'm like you. I'm into Family with a capital "F."*
> *Ours is so small. I like to keep it together as much as*
> *possible. Also like you, I am so anxious to know more*
> *of our history. Alice was my best bet and I guess I*
> *never leaned on her enough to tell me more. My father*
> *surely could have, but 30 years ago, I didn't have that*

much of a drive for information. Even my mother
could have helped, but here we are with little to go by.

Lynne was still very busy designing jewelry for the business she developed with her sister Margie after she closed
the little shop on Lexington Avenue, and she was also pre-
occupied with the declining health of her husband, Al. But
finally, she found the time to dig out her collection of family
photos. She wrote:

> *I'm sending you some of my treasures. The top*
> *one is an afternoon in our backyard in Mt. Vernon*
> *in the months after your mother arrived. I thought*
> *your mother and father look so terrific here, you might*
> *want to have them lifted out into a beautiful picture*
> *of just the two of them.*

I loved the photo of Alice and Fez at Lynne's parents'
home in Mt. Vernon. I could sense the touch of their
bodies, his torso curved around hers, her head tipped
toward his.

The reunion photo arrived at the end of the week, Lynne's
careful script across the top: "Farewell dinner party for the
American Lewins at the home of Max and Nelly, Leipzig
1927." The setting was as she had described—a long, elegant
table with placemats and fine glassware, though I hadn't anticipated the number of people. I had always thought my
mother had a small family, just Alice and Erika, and a bois-
terous older woman we called *Tante* Edith, whom I visited
with my mother at her apartment in Manhattan on rare

occasions or overheard Mom talking with on the phone. In the Leipzig dinner party photo, I counted thirty people, almost all my mother's aunts, uncles, and cousins. Lynne included a photocopy with a number over each person's image corresponding to his or her name at the bottom.

It was strange to see this large, prosperous, multi-generational family—*my family*—yet they were complete strangers to me. The men wore formal tuxedos with black bow ties, many sporting the short mustache that made them look like Hitler. It was disconcerting to see my Jewish ancestors mirroring a style I associated with the Führer. Nelly and Lillian, Lynne's mother, were elegant in straight, glittery dresses, the vogue of the twenties. Alice and Erika, with their bobbed hair and matching checkered dresses, looked like the schoolgirls that they were, Alice thirteen and Erika fifteen. None of them could have imagined that their future was so precarious.

"How in the world do you remember people you met once when you were six years old?" I asked Lynne, incredulous, when I reached her that evening.

"Dad used to talk about his siblings and point them out to me. There were three brothers—Max, (your grandfather), George, and my father, Curtis—and four sisters: Meta, Selma, Paula, and Ellie. I saw some of them again when I was older," she explained. "Aunt Paula came here in the thirties and my father tried to convince her to stay, but she went back to Germany, where her husband was buried. Unfortunately, she ended up in Theresienstadt, where she was blinded and died. The only siblings who survived were Ellie and her husband, who got to Palestine with plenty of

their own money and lots of your mother's and Erika's too—
I told you the story of the dead cows. Also Uncle George
with his wife Ruth and two daughters who Dad brought to
New York."

Lynne's warm voice masked the gravity of her words. I
registered that my mother's Aunt Paula was blinded at Theresienstadt. I had heard of the concentration camp in what was
then Czechoslovakia, and remembered some scenes from a
TV miniseries, *The Winds of War*. The Nazis misrepresented
the camp to the Red Cross and the world as a model Jewish
community with healthy conditions and cultural activities,
while behind the scenes it was a death camp and a transport
point on the way to Auschwitz.

"My father wanted all his siblings to come to New York,
but they had other considerations and stayed in Germany
until it was too late," Lynne explained. "Selma and Meta
and their husbands, both university professors, perished in
the camps. Selma's daughter Ilsa, the smiling young woman
on the far right, escaped to Paris with a Christian family, but
got turned in by someone and was later dragged back and
killed in the gas chambers. Her brother Werner survived
and became a great friend to your mother until he died in
Israel twenty years ago."

I recalled having heard the name Werner from my mother
but I'd never met him. It seemed as though my mother had
two separate lives that didn't cross paths. I hadn't taken any
interest in her other life until after she was dead, and now I
grasped at every scrap of information as though I needed to
reclaim the missing pieces to make my life whole.

But it wasn't easy to digest. Two sisters in fancy gowns

who lost a lot of money was one thing, but it was another to hear that my close relatives died in the gas chambers or were among the piles of dead bodies in World War II newsreels. I didn't want to associate members of my family with the concentration camp victims. It had been more comforting to say, "My parents were lucky they got out so early."

I looked back at the photo and stared at each face as though I could squeeze some answer from the picture. Selma, with her hands crossed on her ample lap and the hint of a smile on her lips looked like a warm, motherly figure. I imagined she would have fared well in the role she expected, but her kindness couldn't save her from conditions no one had ever imagined. Were the people who survived more resilient, more resourceful, or just lucky, I wondered.

When a friend asked me if I was becoming obsessive, I had to laugh. That was an understatement. I was having imaginary relationships with people I didn't know, filling an inner void with relatives and ancestors. Was it a way to put some ground beneath my feet? I was beginning to accept that I didn't spring from a vacuum, and I wanted to understand the forces that shaped me, especially the ones nobody talked about.

My old friend knew me back when I was a rebel who rejected all family traditions and didn't want any part of my mother's inheritance—not even her enameled spoons. I escaped to college and told my roommate that I was the apple who wanted nothing to do with the family tree. Yet now I found myself not only looking for the tree but determined to dig up the roots too, if that's what it took to piece together my ancestry. How naïve I was to think I could slip away unscathed. I didn't understand how much the *unknown* past was woven into my beliefs and expectations. I wondered whether there was anything else to find and if there was, what difference it would make.

Not long afterwards I had an opportunity to take another look at the truth. I was visiting a nursing home with a friend, and the conversation turned to my family research project.

"I have a book," my friend's mother, Hilda, said, "that has the records of every German citizen killed in the camps by the Nazis. They were meticulous record keepers."

I looked at the frail woman, sitting in her wheelchair and leaning slightly to the right to compensate for her painful hip joint. Her comment startled me. Without changing her tone of voice, Hilda leaned forward to bring her face closer to mine and put her hand firmly on my arm.

"Do you want to see it?" she asked, tipping her face upward so I was forced to look directly into her eyes. "You don't have to."

I paused before responding. "Yes. Yes, I do want to see the book," I finally answered.

We went back to Hilda's room to get the book. My friend pushed the wheelchair down the hall as I walked next to her mother. She told us that her family was very active in the Jewish community in Frankfurt, and she used to go to the train station to see people off when they left for Palestine.

"We were teenagers and had a strong bond through Jewish clubs and associations; we were full of hope and idealism. We sang Zionist songs to celebrate those who were going to the 'promised land,' though we didn't know if we would ever see them again.

"I didn't get to Israel until a few years ago. That's where I bought this book."

With her daughter's help, Hilda went to the closet and got out a heavy bound book with a navy blue cover, about ten inches by eight inches. The title read: *Gedenkbuch Berlins der Jüdischen Opfer des Nationalsozialismus*, The Berlin Remembrance Book of the Jewish Victims of National Socialism. It was published in Berlin and documented German Jews from the Berlin area.

"I met a cab driver when I was in Israel who told me about this book," she explained. She paused. "I bought a copy for each of my siblings. The book was expensive."[4]

I looked with awe at the clean, carefully typeset volume. Each entry listed a person by last and first name, sometimes also with maiden name, date and place of birth, date and place of deportation, date and place of death, if known.

I turned the glossy white pages of the *Gedenkbuch*, the Book of Remembrance, to the H section for Selma's married name, Hamburger. The reality of finding her name shocked me. I didn't really expect it to be there.

Hamburger, Selma, geborene Lewin.
Geboren am 04. Oktober 1872 in Glogau.
Deportationsziel: 15. Juni 1942,
Sobibor Vernichtungslager.

Hamburger, Selma, born Lewin.
Born on October 4, 1872, in Glogau.

Deportation destination: June 15, 1942,
Sobibor extermination camp.

A face in a family reunion photo and a few lines of print were all I could find of my great aunt, who grew up in a wealthy, educated family, married a university professor, and had two children. But it was important—a record that Selma Lewin Hamburger's life had existed, and her death.

The listing affected me more than I would have anticipated. I had heard the statistics, six million Jews murdered; but one notation in a commemorative book forced me to picture a woman's journey from a life of comfort and safety to Bendorf-Sayn, an asylum where Jews were imprisoned, then a transport train to Sobibor, an extermination facility.

I could barely sleep that night. I tossed and turned and had terrible dreams that I couldn't reconstruct in the morning. But I did remember a meditation retreat we had attended with a Vietnamese Buddhist teacher named Thich Nhat Hanh. A student asked him if he gave money to beggars and homeless people. His answer was that he did not choose to give them money, but he did look into their eyes, "I look at them with compassion. I do not avert my eyes from their suffering," he said.

The photograph of the Lewin dinner party and the Book of Remembrance had opened a walled place in me. The way I tried to explain it to Michael was: "I can no longer avert my eyes."

19

The Swiss Account

Two more years passed after Uncle Willy's death, and I felt like the trail to my mother's past had grown cold again. Then on the night of June 21, 1995, the phone rang just as we were getting ready for bed.

"Lynne? Is that you?" I looked at my watch and saw it was past midnight in New York. "Why are you still up at this hour?"

"Al was reading the *Wall Street Journal* in bed and saw an article about the Swiss bank accounts. There's pressure on the Swiss government to look into accounts that were never claimed, like your grandfather's."

My heart beat faster. "That's crazy. Why is it coming up now, after so long?"

"They call them dormant accounts. Just get the paper," she said.

"I'll get it in the morning. I can't even imagine...."

The next morning I bought the *Wall Street Journal* and read the article[5]:

Secret Legacies
Heirs of Nazis' Victims Challenge Swiss Banks Over Deposits from World War II Era

For 50 years, since the end of the war, banks here have cast a dismissive blanket of silence over the question of what they did with accounts opened by Jews and others who were then persecuted, and often murdered, by the Nazis....

For Jews to smuggle possessions out of Nazi Germany was both illegal and extremely dangerous. Those who did often gave banks false names, used numbered accounts to disguise their identities or found others to deposit the money for them....

Anyone turning up at a bank with documentary evidence should have no trouble claiming the money, providing that person can prove he or she is the rightful heir. But frequently there simply is no documentation. Some of the unclaimed money falls under the category of "heirless assets," because it belonged to people whose entire families were wiped out. But even when relatives survived, they often don't know which bank was used. They may only have sketchy anecdotal evidence that there is an account at all. As Mr. Levinsky, the Jewish activist, says bitterly: "You didn't take your bank details to Auschwitz and out again." As a result, some of those petitioning the banks have little to go by, their letters providing at most sad personal testimony to the atrocities of the age.

So many people lost far more than my mother. She was one of the lucky ones. Yet I had never acknowledged the value of her paltry treasures—enameled teaspoons, a silver vase, a gold chain that had once been her father's watch fob. I was beginning to understand why someone would cling to an old necklace, a piece of tarnished silver, or the belief in a vanished bank account—the only markers of a lost life.

"I need to pursue this," I said to Michael. "It would be a way to prove that her belief was right, not about the honesty of the Swiss, but in her certainty that her father's bank account still existed. I have a copy of a letter that my mother wrote in 1953 claiming that her father deposited his money in a bank in either Geneva or Lausanne. Can you imagine what was going through her mind?"

In the first years after Alice came to America, the traumas of the past must have paled in comparison to the promise of a bright future. But my father's death shook loose the debris of all that had been destroyed. I saw my mother at the age of thirty-nine, looking around our house and seeing how drab it had become, how threadbare the Persian rugs she'd shipped from Germany in the first trunk Lynne's father picked up, how dull the worn tweed slipcover on the couch. I could imagine her clenching her jaw to hold back the tears of rage, the memories of wealth that dissolved into ash like the books burned in the square in Leipzig, and the precious savings she concealed on her person as she crossed the border into Palestine, now all used up, with nothing to fall back on. It was at this juncture that she made a renewed effort to find the Swiss bank account.

"I used to have a poster of a painting by Diego Rivera, *The Flower Carrier*," I said to Michael. "You know it, the one where the peasant in the picture is bent over with the weight of the large basket bound to his back? His basket was supposedly filled with flowers but you can feel the burden of the pain he carries on his shoulders. That's how I feel. I thought that because I was born in America, I wasn't really affected by the persecution of the Jews or whatever happened to my relatives—not personally—but I was wrong. I do carry the weight of what occurred before I was born."

"That's a lot to take on," Michael said. He meant to be sympathetic, but it also confused him that I was suddenly so absorbed with the issue of my Jewish responsibility.

I could see his perspective. The religion of my childhood had offered little solace in my younger life, and except for attending several bar mitzvah rituals, I had not participated in anything that had to do with the Judaism in all the time Michael knew me. If someone asked me what religion I was, I often said, "My *parents* were Jewish," to separate myself and make clear that I had chosen a different path.

But the issue of Holocaust-era Swiss bank accounts reminded me that I was part of a Jewish community that was bigger than just my immediate family, even if I was not observant of the religious traditions. Whether I called myself Jewish, Buddhist, American, or Californian, I saw this search for truth as part of my heritage.

In April 1996, New York Senator Alfonse D'Amato, chair of the U.S. Senate Committee on Banking, Housing, and Urban Affairs, started hearings in the Senate to put pressure on the Swiss Banking Association to establish a central information department to review and respond to claims for "dormant, heirless assets." In May, the Independent Committee of Eminent Persons, also known as the Volcker Commission, was created by an agreement between the Swiss Banking Association, the World Jewish Restitution Organization, and the World Jewish Congress.

I was stunned by the steady stream of articles about the role of Swiss banks in relation to the Nazis. The Swiss were not just "lucky" that Hitler didn't invade their "neutral" country. In fact, new information revealed that the Swiss sheltered gold and wealth stolen by the Nazis, and profited after the war by keeping unclaimed assets that were not necessarily heirless at all. By October 1996, twelve thousand Holocaust survivors had filed a class action suit against four Swiss banks for the recovery of dormant accounts and looted property.

Sometime later, I saw an article online by an Australian lawyer named Henry Burstyner, who was born in a Nazi labor camp in Poland. He wrote: "In the 1920's and 1930's the Swiss made chocolates, watches and Swiss cheese. Today they are a world financial centre. It is hard to believe that the money used by the Swiss for this transformation was earned by them from the sale of chocolates, watches and cheese!"[6]

In the 1950s, the prevailing wisdom was that you should "keep your problems in your own kitchen." Now, the public forum about the Swiss bank accounts served as an international invitation to change the pattern of silence and secrets. The scale of the international exposé made me feel exhilarated, as though somebody else cared about what happened to my mother—and all the other nameless mothers and fathers—after all. I recalled the words of one German newscaster on the night the Berlin Wall was breached. He described the chance encounter of two old friends, one from East Berlin and the other from the West, as "a coincidental meeting on the edge of history." Now I was coming face to face with my own unexpected meeting with history.

As soon as I found the contact information for the new commission, I called Switzerland and requested a claim form. When the envelope arrived from Switzerland, I tore it open and saw that a claim submission required a fee of 300 Swiss francs—about $250 at that time.

"Those bastards!" said Lynne, when I told her. "It's unconscionable."

I spread the nine-page application from the Swiss Banking Ombudsman on my kitchen table. Except for the birth and death dates I had collected from the Leipzig property documents, and my mother's 1953 letter about an account in Lausanne or Geneva, I still had nothing to substantiate my claim. But I had my instincts and Lynne was on my team. She offered to write a testimonial letter to go with the application and Tom agreed to split the fee.

I added a second letter, from a woman named Sidy Rayfeld who had been a friend of my mother's in Leipzig. I had met Sidy several times when I visited my mother in New York, and she had taken my daughter shopping at Loehmann's and to a Broadway musical.

Sidy was a tiny, vibrant woman whose voice could fill a room. She immigrated to New York after escaping from the Nazis, married a man she had dated in Germany, and had twin daughters. She played the piano and accordion, and her husband, Ziggy, played the violin. They built a career performing together at Jewish weddings and bar mitzvahs, and in clubs in New York and hotels in the Catskill Mountains. After her husband passed away, in 1975, she moved to San Diego and continued to play piano with a performance group called the Forever in Their Primetime Players.

I wouldn't have known Sidy were it not for remarkable bit of synchronicity that brought my mother and Sidy together after almost thirty years.

It happened in 1963, my junior year of college. I was going to study art in Italy, but was not part of an organized program. I was just an adventurous eighteen-year-old who had found very inexpensive passage on a student ship crossing the Atlantic to Genoa. As the ship started to move out into New York harbor, I stood on deck waving furiously to my mother on the dock below. I knew her eyes were as teary as mine, but my anxiety was eased by a friendly word from a girl my age who was waving just as furiously to her mother.

Jackie and I became instant friends on our ten-day transatlantic crossing. We sat together in the dining room, talked as though we had known each other all our lives, and later hitchhiked together from Florence to Paris.

When we arrived in Paris, we found letters from our mothers waiting for us at American Express. Both wrote about finding themselves face to face just as they turned away from the departing ship.

"You are Alice Lewin from Leipzig!" screamed Sidy.

"Sidy Bienenstock!" screamed my mother.

Torn from their past by the Nazis, they had lost each

other. But once they found each other again they remained close friends until my mother's death.

Sidy was very happy to hear from me. I had a conference coming up in San Diego, so I made a plan to have dinner with her. Michael and I went to her modest apartment. A piano took up one corner of the living room and a small dining table pressed up against the window with a distant view of the Pacific Ocean. Her German accent and even her speech intonations were so familiar to me.

Sidy narrowly escaped the Nazis in 1938. The police came to her door one night and ordered her mother and brother to leave immediately for Poland, as they were not German citizens. She was exempt because she had already obtained a visa to go to the U.S. She watched her family leave that night with only the clothes they could carry. Later, coming back to Leipzig from Warsaw, where she had brought her family some belongings, she saw a brilliant glow of light on the horizon over the city.

"It was November 9, 1938," she said, "the terrible night of destruction when the Germans smashed and burned Jewish properties and synagogues—Kristallnacht, the night of broken glass."

Sidy had seen terrible things, but unlike my mother, she willingly talked about her experience. In fact, she had given an interview to the Shoah Foundation for its documentation of stories from survivors of the Holocaust.

"A month later, just as I was about to leave Germany for Rotterdam, to board a ship to America, I was called into the government office for a search of my suitcases. An official pulled out a music book where I had hidden ship tickets

I planned to mail to my mother and brother once I got to America. The official flipped through the book, but the pages where the tickets were secreted stuck together. I stood there with my hands clenched into fists."

She paused and looked away for a moment.

"I had deep red fingernail marks on my palms for days after."

Her last letter from her mother arrived in 1941. She believed her mother and brother both died in the Warsaw ghetto.

I was touched by the frankness of Sidy's account and felt a familial closeness. As we sat drinking tea after dinner, I brought up the Swiss banking issue.

"I heard Alice talk of the Swiss bank account," Sidy said, "and I would be very happy to write a letter if you think it would help."

This is the letter she wrote:

To Whom It May Concern:

I, Sidy Rayfeld, nee Bienenstock, born in Leipzig, Germany, hereby declare:

Alice Feniger, née LEWIN, and I were close friends. We both were born and raised in Leipzig. I knew her family, her father, who was a well-known dentist, her mother and her sister Erika.

Our friendship survived necessary emigration, marriage, divorce, death, and when we both found each other again in the U.S.A., our friendship became even closer.

Alice mentioned many times, that her father had deposited a large amount of money in a Swiss bank account, that this money would have been her and her sister Erika's inheritance, but that all the papers pertaining to this account were lost because of the persecution of the Jews by the Nazis. She tried very hard to attain access to this money, got in touch with bankers and hired lawyers, invested a large amount of money, but all this without success. Had she and her sister been able to receive that money, life for Alice would have been much easier, since she was widowed at a young age and had a hard time raising her two children.

Respectfully,

Sidy Rayfeld

Like Lynne, Sidy considered Alice a dear friend; she listened to her and believed her. It gave me solace to consider that I was not the only one my mother could talk to after all.

∽

On September 20, 1996, I clipped together the application, several documents from the restitution file to show lines of inheritance, the two testimonial letters, and a bank check for 300 Swiss francs. I placed the folded pages in an 8½-by-11 manila envelope. At the post office, I added airmail postage and a Return Receipt Requested label. Before the postal clerk threw my envelope into the outgoing mail bin, I said a little prayer: "May this bring peace to all."

On the way home, I looked up at the sky and saw that the fog was beginning to roll in across the bay.

20

A String of Pearls

For the next few months, I felt a shiver of anticipation every time I stepped out the front door to collect the mail. I imagined myself reaching into the box.... *My fingers fall on a long white envelope with a Swiss return address. I tear it open and read: Your grandfather's bank account has been found.*

But as time passed, my frustration grew. Sometimes I went to the mailbox every hour or two. I chewed on my nails and got increasingly restless until I finally heard the clank of the postman opening and closing the metal lid. When I found just the usual bills, my heart sank like that of a desperate lover waiting by the phone for a call that doesn't arrive.

This was how my mother must have felt when she sent letters and hired lawyers to find her father's account. Now that I knew more of her earlier losses, I could see that my father's death would have struck her like a replay of the disasters she faced in the 1930s, when so many things in her life collapsed, one after another.

I wanted to talk to Tom about the period surrounding my father's death. In October 1996, he had a chance to come to San Francisco for a conference. After his meetings were over, I took him and Harriet to Golden Gate Park for the afternoon. Tom and I sat on a stone bench in the Rose Garden while Harriet walked on ahead to investigate the array of multicolored blossoms.

"How did you find out that Daddy was dead?" I asked.

"I haven't thought about that for a long time," he said after a pause. "It was a couple of days after he went into the hospital. I came downstairs from my bedroom and was hit by a bank of smoke. Mom and Erika were sitting at the kitchen table in front of an ashtray full of half-smoked cigarette butts. Mom turned to me and said, 'You don't have to go to school today. Daddy died.' That was all."

"I had no idea," I said, touched by the poignancy of Tom's situation.

"What did you do?"

"Neither of them reached out to me. No one touched me. I just turned around in a daze and went back up to my room."

My brother's gray-green eyes, so like my father's, looked moist, and I noticed the flecks of light in them. I didn't know if I had upset him, but I needed more. I had returned from Erika and Willy's to a cold, empty house with no transition and no understanding of what happened.

"Was there a funeral?"

"Yes. We all drove to the Montefiori cemetery in Queens. In those days the men cut their ties as a sign of mourning. I guess that was a version of tearing your clothes. I remember that Mom was very upset and didn't want me to cut my tie. She had an argument with Nathan, and insisted on leaving my tie alone."

"Did you?"

"Of course. Mom got her way."

"Who came?"

"It's hard for me to remember the details. I was in shock. I think Cousin Lynne, her husband Al, and her sister Margie. Of course, Nathan and Pearl, and Bill and Erika, were there. Later we went back to the house to sit shiva. More people arrived as the day wore on, the Schweizers, Ilsa Maleniak, even a couple of people from Trylon Realty. You know, their friends from Germany were very loyal. Mom and Dad were the same way. They would always go if someone died or someone was sick. People told stories and we laughed. The adults were very nice to me, and there was lots of food and soda. But I felt bad enjoying myself because it didn't seem right. When everyone left, the house got deadly quiet."

"I wish I could have had a chance to be with all those people and talk about Daddy."

"I know. I don't know why they didn't let you come, but that's the way they did everything. When Opa died, I was ten and away in summer camp. They didn't tell me. I got home at the end of summer and ran upstairs to his room on the top floor to see him and Mom said, 'You don't have to visit him—he died.' I had a shaky feeling, like, what do I do now?"

"Did you ever talk to anyone about Daddy?"

"Not really. Maybe Bill mentioned him once. It was difficult to go back to school the next week as though nothing had happened. Mom wrote a note to explain I missed a day of school because my father had died. What could I say? I felt numb. After Daddy died, the lights went out."

Tom and I sat quietly watching the sun peak in and out from the drifting fog. I put my hand on his shoulder, grateful for a feeling of tenderness we had not shared in a long time.

∽

On January 17, 1997, four months after I submitted my claim, a new discovery shook up the Swiss Banking scandal. The *New York Times* reported that Christoph Meili, a night watchman at the Union Bank of Switzerland, had found two large bins full of documents waiting to be shredded.

> The contents were unmistakably old and they were a jumble: from oversized ledger books with entries handwritten in fountain pen, to decades old contracts, to lists of mortgaged buildings in German cities like Berlin and Breslau in the 1930's and 1940's—the years of Nazi rule in Germany.

> Mr. Meili made a fateful decision that he knew would probably cost him his job: he grabbed an armful of books and papers, took them to a Jewish cultural organization the next day and then went public with what he knew....

> Mr. Meili's action rocked U.B.S., Switzerland's biggest bank, which acknowledged on Tuesday that it had made a "deplorable mistake" and may have

violated a new Swiss law created to protect material that might shed light on the Holocaust.[7]

As I read the article, my throat tightened. I saw a mountain of precious financial records, including Max Lewin's bank account, shredded and ragged, like the newspapers we tore into strips to make papier-mâché masks in elementary school.

The next month I found a letter from the Contact Office of the Swiss Banks in Zurich in the mailbox. This was the response I had waited for over the last five months, and I savored the rush of possibilities it might offer, dreams that ranged from simple peace of mind to buying a home of our own. I held the envelope next to my heart before carefully sliding my letter opener along the edge.

February 10, 1997

Dear Madam,

We must unfortunately now inform that no positive reports were received from any of the banks applied to. This indicates that no dormant accounts (accounts, custody accounts or safe deposit boxes) are held in any Swiss bank under any of the names or designations cited by you.

It only remains for us to assure you that the enquiry was treated with the utmost diligence. We regret that we are unable to give you a more satisfactory reply.

Yours faithfully,

Contact Office of the Swiss Banks

"No!" I screamed to the empty hallway. I screamed for Mom teaching herself shorthand in the New York city rush hour, for Nelly feeling so destitute she couldn't even face her two daughters, and for myself, daring to dream of something beyond my normal expectations.

"We know it was there," Lynne said emphatically, when I called her with the disappointing news. "Hire a lawyer," she said. "Don't give up."

"Oh, Lynne, I'm afraid *my cows died!*"

I couldn't see the point in hiring a lawyer, but at least I knew I wasn't alone in sifting through the ashes of the Holocaust. The paper was full of articles about individuals, organizations, and world leaders who were actively engaged in sorting out the truth about the disposition of Jewish assets, the handling of dormant accounts, and the sale of unclaimed treasures such as art and jewelry.

Later that year, on July 23 (coincidentally my mother's birthday), I spread out the *New York Times* on my kitchen table:

Swiss Find More Bank Accounts From the War and Publish List

Under mounting international pressure, Switzerland's major banks are publishing a list today of roughly 2,000 dormant World War II-era accounts that may include the assets of Holocaust victims. The list names more than twice the number of such accounts that the banks said they had identified as recently as 1996."[8]

It was shocking to see how many names were on the list, how many people never returned to claim their accounts. I scrolled down the list to Levy...Levy...Lewin. This time Max Lewin was on the list.

I decided to call our local newspaper. *The Contra Costa Times* published an article with the headline "Grandfather's Swiss Bank Account Opens Past for Berkeley Woman"[9] and soon after I got a call from a local TV station. A reporter came to our house and took close-up shots of the *New York Times* list and the precious photo of Alice and Erika sitting together on the loveseat.

As Michael and I watched my story on the evening news, I felt exposed and vulnerable. More like my mother than I would like to admit, I have always been alert to any sign of threat or aggression. I suspected that this was more than just my natural temperament, that it had a connection to being Jewish, in particular German Jewish. I observed that Jewish friends whose parents and grandparents were born in America didn't share my paranoia. But this time I was willing to be public, to stand up for the relatives who weren't here to speak for themselves.

As I filled out the required application for a second time, I thought of my mother's resilience despite her losses. I remembered her doing jewelry repairs for Lynne, sitting at the kitchen table in the evening with a bright lamp focused on a square of dark blue quilted cloth. She laid a row of pearls out on the fabric, organized by size, smallest to largest and back to smallest. Slipping the needle and thread through the tiny hole, she flipped the necklace in a graceful gesture that formed a knot between each pearl. Then she pulled the knot

tight between her thumb and index finger to produce a perfectly spaced strand of cultured pearls.

I pictured my mother's face in the glow of the lamp, the
furrow of her brow as she concentrated all her attention on
her work. Now it was my turn to string the pearls of her life
story—to lay them out in chronological order and knot
them back together in a perfect strand.

21

The Settlement

A month after I submitted my second application, the Contact Office of Swiss Banks informed me that my claim was once again denied "on the grounds that the Claimant's grandfather was already dead at the time the account was opened."

This namesake is a coincidence, as there is no concurrence of other data provided by you.

The Jewish Bulletin included my experience in an article about the frustrating hunt for names on the Swiss list,[10] and I was still convinced there was a bank account, but I thought of the shredded documents and didn't have the heart or the will to proceed. Fortunately, some other good news drew my attention.

In September 1997, our lawyer, Mr. Osen, wrote, "The Restitution Authority has issued a preliminary decision awarding reconveyance of the Leipzig property to you." It was seven years since October 1990, when our claim had been filed for possession of 32 Grassistrasse. But Osen added that after the huge infusion of money from the German government ceased, unemployment, business collapse, and the exodus of people who relocated to the west reduced the property values in the former East Germany. *Neue Leipziger,* the development company that had contracted to buy the land, wanted to renegotiate the original purchase agreement. The lawyer proposed a reasonable settlement, and my brother and I agreed to accept the revised terms. It was only a matter of accounting before he would send us our share of the money from the sale.

The news came as I was leaving for Florida to visit Tom and Harriet and to promote my new book, *Journey from Anxiety to Freedom.* In this self-help book, I chronicled the lives of eight different people, including myself, who had struggled with panic attacks and anxiety issues. The book described the different paths each of us followed to regain our confidence.

Just before we left for my book signing, Mr. Osen called Tom and said that he was ready to mail our checks from the sale of the property. Instead of sending mine to California, we asked him to send both checks to Florida. Seventy years after our family's property was taken away by Aryanization, Tom and I would be together to receive the restitution payment. What could be more auspicious? I thought.

Liberties Bookstore in Boca Raton was unusually crowded for a Monday night. When I stepped up to the podium, I looked out at an audience that included my niece and nephews and their friends. Their attentive faces encouraged me, and I talked about my own story, admitting that even though I had been very adventurous in the past, when I started having panic attacks my life shrunk. Normal activities like freeway driving and flying became so filled with dread that I had stopped going anywhere, until I learned how to use relaxation, meditation, and new ways of thinking to reclaim my life.

"The plane trip to New York when my mother lay in a coma, dying, was the first time I flew in six years," I told the audience. I looked toward my brother, and was tempted to say that once again I had come east for a significant, life-changing event, but something held me back.

The next day the doorbell rang, and the postman asked my brother to sign for a registered letter. What a mundane activity it seemed compared to the mixture of emotions it stirred in me: awe, gratitude, and sadness that my mother wasn't with us. I wanted to see her face light up, to hear her breathe a deep sigh of relief and say that life was good and we could all be happy.

"Let's see what we have here," Tom said cheerfully. He opened the envelope, handed me a check made out in my name and walked over to the kitchen counter where he picked up his car keys.

I could feel my face flush.

"Wait a minute," I called out. "What are you doing?"

"I'm going to deposit my check," he said.

It took me a second to find my voice.

"Wait. You can't—Tom, don't go so fast. This isn't just

money. This is a miracle. I need to mark this moment, to acknowledge how this came about."

Tom stopped moving. Harriet and Michael walked toward us, but neither of them spoke. I could feel Michael's presence hovering by my side, and I had a sense that he was holding his breath.

My brother didn't view this as a sacred occasion. His relationship with Mom was different from mine, tainted with hurt and disappointment that he wanted to put behind him. His priority was to meet his son, who worked at a brokerage house, and deposit the check in his account. He turned to me, and asked, "What do you want?"

What I wanted most at that moment was to run away. I asked Michael to come outside with me. The warm, humid breeze on my bare arm felt unfamiliar in the middle of November. I felt out of time, out of place, out of step with myself.

A thread of history pulled me back to Alice and Erika visiting their mother in the hospital, to Erika's husband giving his official approval for the sale of the apartment building that had been the girls' home, two young women packing up remnants of their past and boarding a train, then a ship to go to Palestine to collect the money for their cows— a transaction that was supposed to give them the resources to start a new life in America.

"Try not to get too upset. He doesn't really understand what this means to you."

I heard Michael's voice and felt his arm around me. I exhaled, a long sigh as though I hadn't breathed in months.

"How can it matter so little to Tom?" I said. "I thought

we would both be affected, that it would be some kind of epiphany and bring us closer together."

When we got back to the house, Tom asked if I wanted some lunch. He looked sad and I knew that he didn't want to hurt me. I wasn't hungry but I drank two huge glasses of water. Tom sat on the living room couch and said we could do whatever I wanted. I asked Harriet if she had some candles.

I looked around the room, a living space designed for a hot climate with cool, white tile floors and sparse furniture, set against Tom's colorful oil paintings on every wall. I recognized the familiar Parisian street scene that had hung in their house in New York.

I put four candles in glass holders on a glass table in front of the couch and asked if we could close our eyes and consider the significance of the occasion. Then I lit one candle in honor of Alice, one in honor of Erika, and two to represent our ancestors, known and unknown. I said that the roots of continuity had been severed, and the restitution from our grandparents' home gave us the chance to weave the generations together again.

I imagined my mother's spirit there with us. I had a familiar impulse to soothe my mother, to hold her in my arms and tell her that everything was all right, to be the daughter she addressed in her final note, telling me that she knew I would always take care of her and protect her from evil. But I couldn't make anything happen. I couldn't make her feel safe or convince her to trust life. I wondered if I could still change some of my own patterns of anxiety and distrust. Could restitution of money transform an inherited pattern of insecurity? Could it change the beliefs I passed on to my own daughter?

I blew out the candles.

Harriet said, "Thank you, that was very nice." Then we went in different directions for the rest of the afternoon. Michael and I took a walk on the beach. Later we all sat around the kitchen table and had pasta and salad. We were polite to each other, but I had a bitter taste in my mouth.

That night I barely slept, my rest interrupted by unfamiliar emotions. I was Nelly, enraged at a husband who abandoned her to the Nazis, and Alice, angry at a father who hurt her and a husband who had died and left her alone again. I was every Jewish woman who heard an insistent knock on her door and opened it to find an armed agent of the secret police, the Gestapo, looking for her husband or father. The conclusion I had longed for with such high hopes had arrived, and I wanted to cry.

The night after we returned to San Francisco, I had a dream. The main character was a little boy, but the minute I woke up I knew he was part of me. We had traveled to the Far East, an austere mountain landscape that reminded me of the Himalayas. We were going to see the Master, an old, wise teacher. When we arrived, he handed me a large chocolate bar. "You see," he said, "it cannot be lost. I have always kept it for you."

I understood. It was my inheritance. It was my family legacy. I remembered Uncle Nathan giving me a square of dark, bittersweet chocolate before I went to bed each night. I jumped out of bed and pulled open the curtains to a brilliant blue sky.

Alice and Erika
three and five
Lcipzig 1917

Alice and Erika, ten and twelve, Leipzig 1924

Erika and Alice
fifteen and seventeen
S.S. Bremen 1929

1291

Alice and Erika, seventeen and nineteen, Oberhof 1932

Max and Nelly, Karlsbad 1932

Lewin Family Reunion, Leipzig 1927. Lynne is third child from left.

Alice and Fez
New York
1936

Alice and Fez, Coney Island 1936

Searching at the New Cemetery, Leipzig 2005

Mani at the gravestone of Max and Nelly Lewin, Leipzig 2005

PART THREE

Renewal

What is the thread that holds it all together?
Grief, I thought for a while.
And grief is there sure enough…
But grief is not a force and has no power to hold…
Love is what carries you, for it is always there,
even in the dark, or mostly there in the dark,
but shining out at times like gold stitches
in a piece of embroidery.

Hannah Coulter by WENDELL BERRY

22

A New Home

For two years, the settlement money sat in our savings account. We bought a few new things, a couch and loveseat, a used Jeep Cherokee, but on the surface, life continued as it had been before. However, inside I felt like I had entered a completely new realm. I had a sense of security that was unfamiliar, as though a missing piece of myself had been restored and my feet landed more solidly on the ground. My new roots gave me strength.

In 1999, Michael and I decided to look for a house. By this time his son Key was married and Sarah had her own apartment in San Francisco, so we no longer needed the rambling house we had rented years earlier. We found a modest, two-bedroom in a friendly neighborhood in El Cerrito, just north of Berkeley. The house was built in 1945, the year I was born. It had "good bones" but needed substantial repair. Because of the extent of the work, our realtor asked us to be sure that we really wanted the property even after our offer had been accepted. I was sure.

Our friend Christopher, who had done several renovations with Michael in prior years, before Michael turned in his construction tool belt for a data research job, came to see the house. He paced up and down, then began waving his arms around. "You could knock out this wall, and knock out that, and pop a new window in here." Michael and I looked at each other in dismay, but after he left, we started to fantasize about what we could do. We had never allowed ourselves to dream like that before.

For the next six months Michael worked on the house every evening and every weekend. I remember standing in the gutted house with a broom in my hand, seeing him covered with plaster dust. "I feel like we spent half of your inheritance to buy the house," he said, "and the other half to haul it to the dump." I knew his exhaustion made him wonder if we had gone too far, but I was thrilled with the improvements we were making.

Christopher worked alongside Michael for the whole project. The two of them tore down walls, rewired, painted, and installed new windows, cabinets, and appliances. I dug up the front yard, which had been buried under black plastic and cheap red rocks, picked up debris around the site, and ran around with my camera documenting the transformation. When the building inspector came to check out the finished remodel, he couldn't believe that we hadn't added square footage to the original footprint. The house had changed from a small cottage with dark, tiny rooms to an open design with archways and sliding glass doors that brought in light and sky.

I walked from room to room, marveling at the hard work Michael and Christopher had done. Then I thanked my mother, and felt a new wave of gratitude for the grandparents I never knew. How could I bask in the sunlight that flooded our bedroom in the late afternoon and still harbor resentment toward the source of this inheritance? This cherished house would not let me ignore the role of my grandparents in the circle of renewal that spanned three generations—from a home that was lost to a home restored. My heart felt bigger, as if it could embrace more than before.

An idea came to me: perhaps I could find other people of my mother's generation, her peers, who grew up in Leipzig. Their stories could provide a new window into the landscape of her life and the times she lived in.

I called the *Jewish Bulletin* and referred to the article the paper had published two years earlier, in August 1997, about my grandfather's Swiss bank account. I said that I had not been able to claim my grandfather's bank account, but the experience had shown me that the real treasure was my renewed connection to my family roots. I suggested a follow-up article, and hoped it could help me find some people who had grown up in Leipzig in the 1920s and '30s.

On October 2, 2000, *Jewish Bulletin* reporter Andy Altman-Ohr came to my home. "It doesn't sound like your family had it so bad," he said. "After all, there are some people whose parents died in the camps, or worse."

I agreed with him. "I never thought of my parents as Holocaust survivors, or considered how I was affected by their history. But I'm beginning to understand how my mother's past influenced my attitude towards the future. There was no

point in having dreams; life was so unpredictable, so threatening. Her training was the message of silence," I told Andy,
"and lowered expectations. My intention is to break the silence
and tell the story that was never told." I added that I was seeking anyone born in Leipzig who might talk to me and give me
a sense of the times in which my mother grew up.[11]

Five people contacted me after the paper came out, and
I spoke to all of them. The person who affected me the most
was Dr. Fritz Schmerl, a ninety-eight-year-old man living in
a nursing home in Piedmont, near Oakland. At the end of
his life, he told me about his youth in Leipzig.

Like my mother, Dr. Schmerl loved classical music,
especially Schubert and Schumann. "There were swans in
Augustusplatz," he recalled. "We stood in line on Saturday
morning to get tickets to the opera that evening. When I
was a teenager, I sat on the floor of the gallery following the
words in the libretto."

At the end of one visit, Dr. Schmerl asked me if I would
like to hear a song about a bird who lands on his foot. "Kom-
mt ein Vogel geflogen/Setzt sich nieder auf mein Fuß," he
sang. (A bird comes flying/It sits on my foot.) I understood
a few of the words, and was touched by the last line: "Von
der Mutter ein Gruß" (From my mother a greeting). He
told me it was a song his mother sang to him when he was
a little boy.

My other contact from the *Jewish Bulletin* article, Eve
Wechsburg, was born in Leipzig and immigrated to Los
Angeles in 1939 at the age of seventeen. I spoke with her
several times by phone, and she made my mother's neighborhood come alive in my mind.

In her eighties and full of zest for life, Eve said in spite of the disruption caused by the Nazis, she had many happy memories of her youth in Germany. "Even with what was happening in the outside world," she told me, "my teenage years in Leipzig were full of positive memories. I had a close-knit group of friends who shared dreams of creating a Jewish homeland in Palestine. We were enthusiastic, motivated, and optimistic."

She talked about the neighborhood where my mother grew up, and was the first person to tell me it was called the Musikviertel, Music Quarter, "a very rich and elegant neighborhood." Many of the streets, she said, were named for musicians.

"I took the tram to my piano lessons on Grassi Street," she said, "just a few steps from where your mother lived. I walked past the Reichsgericht, the big, imposing Supreme Court building, then on the next block the world-renowned Gewandhaus Orchestra Hall. One of my most wonderful memories is my sixteenth birthday, when my boyfriend invited me for a dress rehearsal at the Gewandhaus and they played Beethoven's Ninth Symphony."

Eve's reference to the Gewandhaus triggered images of my mother resting on her bed with her radio turned to the classical station, WQXR, listening to concerts performed by the Leipzig Gewandhaus Orchestra. What was she thinking when she heard the announcer speak of a place that was once just a short walk from her home? Did she ever pause for a moment and wonder how her life might have turned out differently? She had no greater passion than her love for classical music. I was certain she attended concerts as regularly as a child today goes to the movies.

The next time I spoke with Eve, I asked what she did for fun and where she bought her clothes.

"When we were teenagers, we went to a beautiful park, the Rosenthal, where we played and flirted with the boys. In the spring, I walked there with my grandfather and we fed the ducks and swans in the pond. In winter it froze and we went ice-skating.

"My mother had many of her clothes custom made by a seamstress, but my clothes came from the store. There was a famous business, Bamberger and Hertz, that sold menswear all through Germany. Ludwig Bamberger was a close friend of my parents. I bought my favorite winter coat at Bamberger's—a blue herringbone tailored men's coat." She paused and cleared her throat. "The Nazis burned down the Bamberger store in Augustusplatz on Kristallnacht. There's a plaque to mark where it once stood."

Eve had witnessed the destruction and violence to Jewish-owned properties on the night of broken glass, yet she had not lost her faith in life. I asked her what happened to her that night. She promised to tell me another time but never did. She said only, "We were very lucky to get out. By 1939, the law was that Jews were not allowed to take anything with them, not silver, nor valuables, nor money."

Eve was only eight years younger than my mother, and it was easy to imagine Alice crossing her path in Leipzig. In my mind, I saw them brush against each other as they tried on fine, woolen coats at Bamberger's, or when they passed each other getting on and off the streetcar at Grassi Street.

They skated by each other on the frozen pond in the Rosenthal, and rubbed shoulders in the lobby of the Gewandhaus Orchestra Hall.

It had been so long since I heard my mother's voice. The remnants of Eve's remaining German accent evoked warmth and familiarity. I just wanted to keep talking, about anything, but she told me she was done, so I thanked her and reluctantly hung up. I wondered why one woman had seen destruction but kept her faith in life, while another, my mother, became cynical.

The conversations with Eve and Dr. Schmerl added color and texture to the tapestry of my mother's life in Leipzig. It was as though Alice and Erika had stepped out of the framed photograph to walk on the streets of the Music Quarter with well-dressed men and women coming and going from the concert hall. They strolled hand in hand in Augustusplatz, throwing crumbs to the swans on their way to the opera. They went shopping at Bamberger and Hertz, and sat on the benches in the Rosenthal whispering to each other about the boys playing soccer on the grass.

As I imagined these scenes, I had no idea that my mother's history would soon come to life in yet another form, and that a vision of her youth from twelve to eighteen would be revealed to me—*in her own hand.*

23

Alice's Photo Album

I shivered as I held the fragile treasure in my hands—just 6 by 9 inches, sepia-toned memories on stiff brown paper, with three or four images on each page. These were the photographs my mother had chosen to preserve, vignettes of the life she once wanted to remember.

Tom had found Alice's buried photo album when he was sorting through more boxes in his garage. Knowing how important it would be to me, he sent it off right away. It occurred to me that maybe I was fortunate he didn't share my fascination with our mother. He had no desire to hold onto anything of hers.

I opened the cover made of teal blue card stock and carefully turned the pages, some with cracked edges or pieces broken off at the corner. A translucent sheet of onionskin covered each page to protect photos held in place by glue or tiny paper triangles. I ran my fingers under the captions below each snapshot, white pencil against a dark background. The vertical script reminded me of letters I got from my mother over a lifetime—sent to summer camps, college dorms, apartments, European American Express offices when I was traveling, and to my home in California, until her last note on Mother's Day 1987.

Why didn't she ever show this album to me? When my daughter Sarah was making plans to go to Europe after college, I couldn't stop myself from telling her stories of my adventures, whether she was interested or not. But my mother never said, "When Erika and I were teenagers, we went skiing in St. Moritz in the Swiss Alps in winter, and boating in Zell am See in the Austrian Alps in summer." But now I could see that they had.

I would have been fascinated by the exotic names of the resorts she frequented and surprised at her contemporary sense of style—skirts just above the knee, bathing suits and shorts rolled up that exposed her whole leg, and ruffled feminine sundresses with spaghetti straps. And I would have pointed to the unfamiliar people and asked who they were. I wondered if that was the very reason she hid the evidence of her prior life. She would have been forced to say that the woman with the fur stole around her shoulders was her mother, or the man walking with a cane, the trousers of his suit hiked up over his belly, was her father. Is it possible she actually forgot the existence of the photographs from that period, as though they belonged to someone else's life, no longer to hers?

Voracious, I devoured a collage of fleeting impressions that spanned the years from a twelve-year-old Alice with a classic cloche hat pulled low over her forehead at Blankenberghe, a popular beach resort on the Belgian coast in 1926, to Lausanne, where she and Erika went to boarding school in 1931.

She was always with Erika, and often among carefully dressed young men with hair parted in the middle or slicked at the side, and girlfriends with scribbled names I had never heard—Liesel, Elsie, Friedel, Bly. One I did recognize, with a start, Annalie, who had told me that she wouldn't talk about those who weren't there to defend themselves.

What was Alice thinking as she sat at the wheel of a Daimler convertible in Marienbad, a resort in Czechoslovakia? What were Alice and Erika laughing about as they skied cross-country in Oberhof, a German town still famous for its winter sports?

A series of photos taken on the deck of the *S.S. Bremen* recorded Alice's trip to England for her fifteenth birthday. In the first picture, her arm is linked through Nelly's and her head is resting on Nelly's shoulder. I hadn't expected to see any sign of affection with her mother. It made me wonder if Alice's relationship with her was not always as harsh as the impression she gave me.

On the next page, Alice is posing with her sister on the ship's deck. Erika wears a belted coat with a scarf thrown casually around her neck; Alice's erect posture and hand on hip convey boldness. She looks contemporary in a striped pullover, blazer, and wraparound skirt. She carries a small shoulder purse with long straps and a beret pulled low on her forehead.

Online, I found a brochure for the ship: "Its unsurpassed speed created the initial wonder, but just as wonderful were the reports of the luxurious appointments, the marvels of engineering, and the gaiety of its distinguished shipboard life." The *Bremen* transported many famous people from its maiden voyage on July 16, 1929, into the 1930s—Marlene Dietrich, Cary Grant, Greta Garbo, even Winston Churchill. A caption in black ink under the photo told me that Alice and Erika were on the maiden voyage: "Auf der Bremen vor England 17 juli 1929."

They must have loved the gala send-off. Journalists and the public crowded the dock, hoping for a sighting from its illustrious passenger list. I imagined Alice and Erika waving wildly from the deck, as though they too had acquired fame by their participation in the event. Later, they strolled past men and women sitting in wicker chairs in the sunroom, sipped champagne with new friends under potted palm trees, or laughed together on the plush loveseat in their stateroom. I could see them that evening as they walked down the grand staircase that led from the balcony down to the dining hall. Many pairs of eyes would have turned their way, two tall, slender, dark-haired young women, just fifteen and seventeen, whose demeanor belied their young ages.

The ship's glamour evoked images of the *Titanic,* but fortunately it hadn't achieved that ship's morbid fame. It did leave its mark on history for the Erster Deutscher Katapultflug, the first German catapult plane. It carried transatlantic "airmail" that was catapulted off the ship before it reached New York, thus allowing the ship-to-shore mail to arrive fourteen hours ahead of the actual ship.

Lynne remembered that "Alice wore diamonds from knuckle to knuckle" when she arrived in New York. But even Lynne's stories didn't impress upon me the affluence of her earlier life until I saw the photos. The woman who made this album came from an upper tier of society. I fantasized about how she and Erika would have been described in the society pages of *Vogue,* or the 1920s German equivalent:

The Lewin sisters, Alice and Erika, were seen Saturday night at a gala ball for the opening of Wagner's *Tannhäuser* at the Leipzig Opera House. Alice wore a fitted gown of tiered cream chiffon; Erika entered the hall in a floor length evening dress of blue silk.

I believed that I had found my mother's brightest years in this haunting album, the magical era of her life when she had the opportunity to savor the pleasures and passions of coming of age. But as I looked at the photos she had secreted away, I felt an ache in my chest, an uncomfortable mix of sadness and anger, realizing that she withheld from me the precious pearls of her youth.

Then I turned the page.

24

Alice and Fez

I stared at young Alice. She was on an outing to the countryside with Erika, Willy, Fez, and a fellow named Ernst Fisher who had been a close friend of both my father and mother. The caption at the bottom of the page said, "Wir!!! in K, Mai '31." *Wir* meant we. I could not identify the place, but the three exclamation marks told me it was no ordinary event for my mother.

"This is another missing piece of the puzzle!" I called to Michael as I pulled him back to the table and pointed to a photo of Alice and Fez lying on the grass, his arm around her shoulder, her head on his chest. "I can't believe she already knew him. She was only sixteen here."

"What can't you believe? Willy told you that your parents went out together in Germany and that your mother wanted Fez from the start."

"Yes, he did, but I didn't get the whole picture. I didn't realize how young and innocent she was when she first met him. Here she is, a young girl, out with an older man, a college student. Let me see—1931—he was twenty-four in this picture."

I saw a girl becoming a woman, naked in her excitement, discovering new feelings, especially for a man called Fez, eight years older. I saw her without the shield of armor that had always protected the mother I knew.

"Your father looks lighter here than in any of the later pictures," Michael observed pointing to another photo of Fez, Willy, and Ernst. My father was laughing, and Willy had a bandage above his left eye, presumably from a fencing injury.

"Yes, of course my father was different then. He had few responsibilities except attending his university classes and dropping by the fur business on Friday so Nathan could give him a paycheck, at least according to Willy, who sounded pretty envious, by the way."

I was obsessed with the people in the photos. I wanted to be one of them, to hear their conversations, to eat their bread, to be as carefree as they were and to feel the earth under their bodies. What happened later shouldn't cancel out the reality of these happy moments, I thought.

Carried on the waves of Beethoven's Piano Sonata No. 23, known as the *Appassionata,* I saw the embryo of my mother's past come to life in the photographs with the men who awakened her to love.

The real change began when Erika met Willy during her last year of high school. She soon started spending all her available time with him and his closest friends, who attended the University of Leipzig with him. Alice, though

younger, was included. They sat at the corner table at Auerbach's Keller near the university and drank Gosé, a unique
beer that originated in Leipzig. They sipped strong coffee at
Kaffeebaum, their ideas and dreams interweaving with the
circling wisps of cigarette smoke, getting heavier and heavier in the room as the night wore on. They walked in the
park on Saturdays, took the tram to the Rosenthal to watch
the swans or sit on the benches to laugh at nothing but the
thrill of being young and free. They met on Thursday eve-
nings to see a performance of Beethoven or Schumann at
the Gewandhaus, and once took in a dress rehearsal of *La
Traviata* at the Opera House, though Fez was not an opera
fan and went out before the intermission to have a smoke in
the lobby.

Unlike the rich, well-tailored boys who came to parties
at Grassi Street and shook her father's hand, these men answered Alice's longing for wildness and passion. She joined
in the intellectual conversation, the heated political debates,
the dueling of ripe minds, and the dawning sensuality that
they, several years her senior, triggered in her. With their
presence in her life, the frustrations with her family, even
her father's temper and her mother's disinterest, receded
into the background.

What began as a group of friends evolved into romantic
rendezvous. Willy's eyes followed Erika's every gesture and
she drank in his every word. He'd been born in Warsaw and
had come to Leipzig to further his studies at the university.
He was handsome and muscular, self-confident and protec-
tive. His voice had a warm, velvety quality. Ernst was serious, studious, and funny. His glasses perched on his forehead

when he wasn't reading; he could keep the others engaged in some philosophical argument long after their thoughts had wandered to food and beer. More reserved than the other two men, he could be counted on for his loyalty and sincerity. He was quite taken with Alice, and she enjoyed his attention.

However, it was Fez who had the magnetic pull on her. He was an intriguing man, warm yet elusive. An idealistic and articulate law student, his demeanor was more that of a poet, a dreamer. His mood could shift in just a look or a word—one moment intimate and charming, the next quiet and remote, lost in some reverie of his own. Behind his liquid gray-green eyes lived mystery. No matter how much he told her, she felt there was so much he didn't say. Women were always attracted to Fez, seeking his attention, but no one woman could really claim him.

In May 1931, Alice, Erika, Willy, Ernst, and Fez went hiking together in the woods at K!!! The day was gorgeous, clear cloudless blue with no sign of the Leipzig cold and gray skies that could persist even through April. The girls wore short-sleeve cotton print dresses with wide belts to accent their narrow waistlines. Alice felt independent, expectant, vulnerable. After eating their dark bread with Gruyere cheese and sliced liverwurst, the friends reclined together on the soft, fragrant grass. She curled up on her side and lay her head on Fez's chest; she was stirred by the warmth of his arm around her back.

The ravages of the Nazis tore this circle of close friends apart. The miracle is that they found each other again in a new world. The passion of these photographs was what Alice had expected to rekindle when she met up with Fez in New York. She must have expected Fez to be the much-sought-after man she knew in Leipzig. But by 1936, neither of them was the same anymore, with too much left behind and all they had been through.

As I turned each page of my mother's album, I pictured my mother leaning over my shoulder, her heart touched by the images of her youth. But she wasn't sentimental. I was the one whose tears blurred the edges of the pictures. Outside my dining room window, the sun passed behind a cloud. I watched as a shadow fell over the backyard, and then the sun returned and made the leaves of the bamboo tree shimmer.

25

The Journey

Over the last few years, I had learned to use the Internet as a source of information. Searching through legal and historical documents, I found records of the transatlantic crossings that brought to America not only my mother, but my father, Erika and Willy as well. The manifests with their immigration details told a compelling story that was far from whatever Tom and I had imagined in our childhood.

Manifest of Alien Passengers

S.S. BERENGARIA
Southampton, England, 20 March 1935
Arrival in New York, 27 March 1935

Feniger, Jakob, 28 years old, single
OCCUPATION: business, able to speak English,
citizen of Germany
RACE: Hebrew
BIRTHPLACE: Gelsenkirchen, Germany
LAST PERMANENT RESIDENCE: Leipzig, Germany

S.S. BERENGARIA
Cherbourg, France, 11 March 1936
Arrival in New York, 17 March 1936

Lewin, Alice, 21 years old, single

OCCUPATION: nil, able to speak English,
citizen of Germany

RACE: Hebrew

BIRTHPLACE: Leipzig, immigration papers issued in
Jerusalem, 11 February 1936

LAST PERMANENT RESIDENCE: Berlin, Germany

S.S. QUEEN MARY
Cherbourg, France, 14 October 1936
Arrival in New York, 19 October 1936

Wojewoda[12], Erika, 23 years old, married

OCCUPATION: housewife, able to speak English,
citizen of Palestine

RACE: Hebrew

BIRTHPLACE: Leipzig, immigration papers issued in
Jerusalem 28 Sept 1936

LAST PERMANENT RESIDENCE: Tel Aviv, Palestine

S.S. HANSA
Hamburg, Germany, 4 Feb 1937
Arrival in New York, 13 Feb 1937

Wojewoda, Wladislas, 28 years old, married

OCCUPATION: farmer

RACE: Hebrew

BIRTHPLACE: Warsaw, Poland

LAST PERMANENT RESIDENCE: Tel Aviv, Palestine

I called Lynne to tell her what I had found.

"I know why you didn't remember seeing Erika when you went with your father to pick up Alice at the pier," I said.

"What are you talking about?" Lynne asked, obviously caught off guard by my unexpected comment.

"Alice was alone. She came all the way from Palestine without Erika. I found the ship records of their passage to America. Alice came in March of 1936, and Erika didn't get here until October, seven months later—and she was pregnant!"

"You're kidding. I don't remember that."

"And you were right about my father. Dad came first in September 1935, a whole year before Mom. Funny, they both took the *Berengaria*. He must have felt so lost here without any members of his family and probably no friends."

Lynne agreed. "Alice gave your father our address, and he visited us at our home in Mt. Vernon soon after he arrived. I don't recall the conversation, but I do remember after dinner my father took Fez into the den for 'men talk.' I bet Dad wanted to hear all about Leipzig. They had many glasses of schnapps together and spoke for hours in German. My father smoked a cigar while your father lit up his pipe. My nose still twitches when I remember the smell of sour cigar smoke mingled with the aromatic pipe tobacco."

"The chronology of their passages to America pulls the whole story together," I said. "My father's in America, on his own, and here comes a girl—now a woman—whom he 'dated' in Leipzig. They speak the same language, they have close friends in common, and sentimental references that make them feel connected. Was she the woman he would have fallen in love with if circumstances had been different? Maybe not. But he feels close to her, and he lets himself enjoy the relationship. He even convinces himself that he's in love, but doesn't think through all the consequences."

Vivid images from photographs of Alice and Fez in 1936 filled my mind: buying hot dogs from a street vendor in Coney Island, walking barefoot on Brighton Beach at the edge of Brooklyn, having a picnic in the woods at Riverside Park.

"Remember," I told Lynne, "Fez was uprooted from his relatively carefree life as a law student. His brother Nathan didn't arrive until 1938, according to the ship records, and his other seven siblings scattered to Italy, Israel, and even Argentina."

I hadn't paused to breathe through my whole monologue and Lynne hadn't made a sound. Finally I let out my breath.

"It's sad," said Lynne, "because your mother really loved him so much in the beginning. She deserved to have a husband who really wanted her."

Her voice dropped at the end of her sentence and I heard a deep sigh. I knew she was thinking of her own marriage. I remembered visiting her at their beach house on Long Island. I noticed how Al hovered around her and rested his hand on her arm. He laughed when she told a story, his eyes focused on her face as though he was hearing a charming anecdote for the first time. She had been fortunate to marry a man who adored her, but the last half year had been very hard. Al had passed away from heart disease earlier in 2002, and though Lynne remained close to her two grown-up daughters, she had lost the spring in her step.

I waited a few seconds but had to go on. "Lynne, can I tell you a little more about these records?"

"Sure, honey. I love all the details. I wish you could find those trunks that the girls sent to the family of Ralph Rotholz. Have you tracked down any clues yet?" she asked.

"Not yet, but I have a friend who is helping me do research." Lynne was more obsessed than I was about what was in the two trunks that the Rotholz family would not give to her father when he drove up to Nyack to reclaim them. I promised to keep looking.

"But for now, can I tell you about the rest of the story as I see it? Look at this," I said to Lynne, who of course could not see through the phone to examine the papers I had pulled out of my files and spread on the kitchen table. "They sold the Leipzig property in December 1935, and by March 1936, Alice was in New York. No wonder she had no love for Israel. She was in Tel Aviv for less than three months and lost her sister, at least temporarily. When Erika met Willy on the street in Tel Aviv, that was the end of twenty-one years of inseparable sisterhood."

Lynne began to say something but I interrupted her. I just had to get the rest out.

"Lynne, there's more. Let me finish. Erika also came alone. The records from the *Queen Mary* show that Erika and Willy were married by then. On the passenger list, she used his last name, Wojewoda, and described herself as a housewife. My cousin was born in April 1937. That means Erika married Willy in Palestine and was four months pregnant when she left him to go on to New York. She was seven months pregnant by the time he joined her."

I paused for a second, trying to imagine what it was like to have such a whirlwind of changes in one year. But I had one more thing to run by Lynne.

"Get this. Alice got pregnant with Tom one month after Erika arrived in New York. One month! Is that an accident? I don't think so. Her sister was married and pregnant, and I don't think she was going to be left behind—Erika and Willy, Alice and Fez, two sisters with two best friends. I don't know if it was all that contrived but on some level...." I knew I was speaking in a rush, but I couldn't stop. So many puzzle pieces seemed to be falling into place.

"I don't blame Mom, or my Dad," I said. "Look, I'm glad Tom and I are here. But it's pretty wild, isn't it? Willy arrives February 13, 1937. Fez tells his best friend that Alice is pregnant. He goes to see your parents and paces and smokes the whole night. Eleven days after Willy's arrival, Alice and Fez get married. There it is. That just about completes the story I was searching for."

"Oh," said Lynne softly. I had never before left her speechless.

Even after I hung up the phone, with no more words left, I couldn't put the subject down. I was haunted by the names printed on the passenger lists and the poignancy of the story they told.

Winter would still have lingered as Alice hung over the rail of the *S.S. Berengaria* to watch the pattern of windswept waves in the ship's wake. This time she is not on a birthday cruise with her sister. She reflects on the events of the last six months and how she had tried to convince Erika to decline the proposal from Rotholz. But Erika could find something good in the most annoying person and she'd seemed so desperate for an adult to tell them what to do.

After the sale of the Leipzig property, they had packed up their most valued possessions and shipped them to the Rotholz family in upstate New York. Then all three went to stay at Ralph's apartment in Berlin until they could arrange passage to Palestine to collect the money from the sale of the cows.

Now she is without her sister for the first time in her life. The cold sea breeze sends a chill up her spine. It was terribly hard to leave without Erika. They had always planned to travel to America together, to live together in New York, to be best friends for the rest of their lives. But when they met Willy on the street in Tel Aviv, all that changed, overnight. The marriage to Willy took her sister away from her. He could not obtain a visa for the United States right away, and Erika chose to stay with him.

Alice is resilient and determined to make a good life in America, and grateful that Uncle Curtis and Aunt Lilly will be waiting at the port. She looks beyond the churning seas and sees a city with modern buildings and infinite possibilities. She decides to be brave and not show how sad she is. She turns back toward the deck and walks to the dining room for a cup of tea.

Shortly after Alice's arrival in New York, Aunt Lilly plans a dinner and invites Fez to join them. How glad he is to see Alice. It warms his heart to hear her Saxon German and see her sparkling dark eyes. He does not formally invite her out on a date. It is just obvious from the start that they are already together. He spends the weekend at Mt. Vernon and doesn't leave her side.

They each have a hollow place they cannot fill. He thinks of his family and sometimes dreams of Annalie, who is still in Germany. Alice misses Erika. But they find pleasure and solace with each other. They go to a concert at Carnegie Hall. It is not quite the Leipzig Gewandhaus but the people are elegantly dressed and the couple in the row behind them are speaking German. Alice cranes her neck to hear them. The woman is from Hamburg and has not been able to get her parents to leave their home. Her father has a shop and does not want to give up everything he has built.

Alice feels her chest tighten. She reaches her hand up to her throat and touches the links of a gold chain wrapped twice around her neck. It was once her father's watch fob. She remembers seeing her father walking with her mother at Karlsbad. He is wearing a bow tie in the photo she took. "This is all that is left of them," she thinks, and a dark cloud starts to form in her mind.

She is relieved to be pulled back to the concert hall by the dimming of the house lights. Fez puts his hand on her leg. The Debussy program conducted by Arturo Toscanini is fabulous. Afterward they drink tea and eat apple cake at the Russian Tea Room.

They don't discuss their future. They both sense that these days are a special time, a bridge suspended between a past gone forever and a future not yet seen. The uncertainty fuels their passion, the heat and spark of the moment fills places recently left vacant.

When Erika arrives on the *Queen Mary* in October, she is almost four months pregnant. Alice wraps her arms around her and cries for joy, but her pleasure is dimmed by her jealousy of Willy. She fears Erika's marriage threatens their private immutable bond. Erika tries to reassure her. "Soeurchen," she says, "don't worry. We will all be together now." She eagerly waits for Willy to get his papers, but it is three more months before he boards the *S.S. Hansa* in Hamburg for his passage to New York.

Fez does not speak to Alice of marriage. His heart was damaged by childhood rheumatic fever, and he has always believed that he will die young and should not have a family. But he doesn't fight the current that is carrying him and Alice deeper into the unknown ocean of their life together.

One month after Erika arrives, Alice notices the change in her body. At first it is a gnawing sensation in her abdomen. Soon the smell of string beans makes her nauseous. Alice's pregnancy is confirmed by the doctor at three months. She does her best to be stoic and ignore the new sensitivity but is unnerved that she cannot control her body as she always has. She feels vulnerable, and wonders for a moment if she and Fez are ready. But they have been so happy together and she believes that he will rise to the occasion.

She tells Fez just days before Willy arrives. Marriage and children were not part of his plan. He stays up all night smoking one cigarette after another and talking with Lynne's parents, Curtis and Lilly, and by morning he has made a decision.

Alice and Fez are married in a private civil ceremony attended only by Erika and Willy. Alice wears a dark navy dress with large white polka dots and a long sweater-coat with a flower that Fez bought pinned to her lapel. Fez is in a wool double-breasted suit with shoulder pads, a silk shirt and tie. Afterward the two couples go out for dinner.

In April 1937, Erika gives birth to a daughter, and she and Willy move to their own place. Alice and Fez rent an apartment on Ocean Avenue in a section of Brooklyn called Flatbush. There are many German Jews already living in their neighborhood, and it's easy to invite friends over for a game of bridge, marble cake and coffee. Erika and Willy often come too, and the two sisters are happy to clear away the dishes and hover over the sink together. Alice washes the plates and cups and hands them to Erika to dry, though neither of them pays much attention. They talk about everything and nothing, nourished by the smell of coffee and their own physical proximity.

In August 1937, Alice and Fez welcome a son. Soon after Tom's first birthday, they move in with Erika and Willy in a house the latter purchased in Laurelton, on the outskirts of Queens.

Alice rarely thinks about the past, though sometimes just as she is falling asleep, she has a flash of memory—an image of her mother, agitated and remote, pacing back and forth across the bedroom floor, or of coming home from school that awful day and seeing blood on the sidewalk. For a moment she is jolted by these visions, but they come less and less often, and she is happy with her life. She is becoming an American, with a husband she loves and a little baby son. Her life is unfolding once again as if by destiny.

26

Ralph Rotholz

I knew very little about Erika's first husband. Willy had told me that he was older, a doctor, and Erika had told her children that her ex-husband had "jumped off the Empire State Building." It was a horrifying image, but I probably would have forgotten about Rotholz had it not been for Lynne urging me to find information about the two missing trunks that the Rotholz family bitterly refused to relinquish to her father almost sixty years ago.

"Whatever was in those two trunks is yours," Lynne repeated every time we spoke. "Your mother went to court, but the family claimed that the contents of the trunks belonged to them. Thank god my father was able to collect the first trunk before they found out that Erika left him."

"But Lynne," I reasoned, "after all this time, who would even remember what was in the trunks, let alone return them to me? Maybe our best shot is to see if the court has any evidence on record about the case or the contents. I'd just like to know what Alice and Erika chose to send to America."

I tried to imagine what went on in my mother's mind as she pared down the belongings of a lifetime into three trunks. Did she choose carefully or just throw in anything that might have value? I pictured the enameled spoons and the silver candy dishes she once tried to give me, a few small rugs and a set of silverware we used when we lived in Jamaica. When Tom gave the set back to me I was surprised by the beauty of the pieces, the engraved initials of a large L with M and N on either side. They must have been used at the home on Grassistrasse for the family reunion when Lynne visited. I noticed that many of the forks were bent and remembered using them to pry open tuna fish cans. I knew they came from Europe and to me they seemed too clumsy and old-fashioned. When my mother remarried, they disappeared and I had never thought of them again, until now.

Tracking down the ancient trunks seemed like an impossible task, so I called on the help of my computer-savvy friend Terri, who had been helping me with research. What she unearthed went far beyond my expectations.

"I haven't been able to find anything about the trunks yet," she told me the following week, "but I'm in touch with a man named Jim Mahoney, the director of the Nyack Library. He's spent years researching his own family genealogy and wants to help you. Can you send him all the information you have?"

The next day I emailed Jim the little I knew about the trunks—their point of origin in Berlin and speculation that they would have been sent around the end of 1935 to some member of the Rotholz family in the vicinity of Nyack, New York.

Within a few days, he sent an article from the *New York Times* dated July 13, 1936. The headline alone sent chills down my spine: "Exiled Physician Ends His Life Here: Dr. Ralph Rotholz, Who Once Had Prosperous Practice in Berlin, Drinks Poison."

> Dr. Ralph Rotholz, 39 years old, who came to this country four months ago from Berlin to escape Nazi restrictions that left him penniless and wiped out a once lucrative practice, committed suicide yesterday morning by swallowing poison in a drug store about half a block from his home, 1166 Gerard Avenue, the Bronx.[13]

The article said that Rotholz left his sister's apartment to make a phone call. He entered the Gerard Drug Store and began a conversation with Abraham Snitofsky, the proprietor, with whom he had gained an acquaintance since his arrival in this country. Snitofsky told police that Rotholz appeared to be in a jovial mood and that he seemed particularly optimistic over resuming his practice soon.

When a customer entered the store, Snitofsky left the prescription room, where they were talking, and walked to the front of the store. When he returned, he found Rotholz slumped against the counter in the rear, a large bottle of poison clutched in one hand. Noting that he was still conscious, the druggist carried the physician to a taxi cab and rushed him to the Morisania Hospital, two blocks distant. But Rotholz was dead when the doctor examined him.

The article stunned me. The Empire State Building story

was dramatic, a sinister echo of the circumstances of Nelly's death. But this revelation of the actual circumstances forced me to see Ralph Rotholz in a more sympathetic way, a man whose suffering drove him to a terrible end. His sister was quoted as saying he was in excellent health, but his actions told a poignant story of a man who could not reassemble a sense of himself or his place in an uncertain world.

A few days later, I got another email from Jim Mahoney. He still hadn't found any evidence of the shipment of trunks, but he included two references to the probate of Dr. Rotholz's estate. The first notice, under "Wills for Probate," was dated October 3, 1936. It indicated that the administration of his estate was assigned to his brother Joseph Holz (an Americanized version of Rotholz?) in Geneva, New York, about 200 miles from Nyack.

The second notice was dated almost two years later, May 26, 1938, and was listed among estates appraised by the Bronx County Surrogate Court. It listed four brothers, two sisters, and a niece and nephew by name. Jim said I might be able to find probate records at the Surrogate Court.

It soon became clear that to find the documents, I would need to go to New York. We were invited to a friend's wedding in Brooklyn in October 2002, and I seized the opportunity to plan a search for records. I also wanted to visit Lynne again. Time was passing. She was in her eighties now and had started to walk with a cane.

Jim Mahoney was not the first, or the last, stranger who stepped forward to assist in my search. In fact, it seemed as though at every turn help came from people I hardly knew.

I spoke to an attorney in New York who had once given

me some legal advice. He offered to send his paralegal assistant to the Bronx Surrogate Court to request the Rotholz file from the archives. A week later he let me know that the records were available. All I needed to do was call the court clerk and tell her when I would be there.

The social events surrounding the wedding kept us busy for the first part of our visit, but in the back of my mind, I counted the hours and minutes until I could get to the Bronx. Finally, the day arrived. Michael and I had lunch with Lynne and took the subway up to Grand Concourse. By the time we exited the subway station, it was pouring rain, with a brisk wind blowing water into our faces. We walked the two blocks to the courthouse and followed directions to the Surrogate Record Room on the third floor. My clothes were soaked and the cold corridor did little to relieve my chill, but I was restored by the warm greeting of the clerk behind the desk.

"We expected you much earlier today," she said.

I had not been able to tear myself away from Lynne and now I noted that the clock on the wall read almost four. "I'm so sorry," I said. "I hope we're not too late."

"Here it is," she said. She pulled a legal-sized file out from under the counter and handed it to me. "There's a copy machine over there that takes quarters." She pointed to the other side of the room. "You cannot remove the file from this office, but you can copy whatever you want."

The package had a musty smell, the file folder crushed and bent by the years it had spent untouched, stuffed in a box on a shelf in the courthouse basement. I sat on the bench and began turning pages. It was awkward and time-consuming to maneuver the thick folder to make copies, and I knew the minutes were passing too fast. Michael, wet and tired, did his best to help me with the copying, but he grew impatient while I nervously read pages clipped together at the top, anxious and afraid I might miss something significant. I labored through the first dozen pages, noting references to the family members in the newspaper probate listing, and found nothing informative. Then I came to the papers entitled "My Will" and read:

> As I have brought divorce-suit against my wife because of improper behavior, I state herewith, that she inherits nothing.

"Improper behavior" like a child who has not shown good manners. I saw the pain in Ralph Rotholz's words, the hurt feelings, the anger. His successful professional life was violently interrupted, derailed by the Nazis. His young and beautiful wife ran off with her former lover. His life had crashed on the rocks once again.

The rest of the will had just two paragraphs listing his brothers and sisters as heirs, and a distribution of one hundred pounds each to three others—a doctor in London, a doctor in Tel Aviv, and a child named Fritzi Kohlhagen, daughter of his dear friend Gustav.

I handed the bulky file to Michael to copy the page with the will, hating to surrender the precious information and all too aware of the clock on the wall. Michael made the copy and then had to go down the hall to change more bills into quarters. I turned the next pages.

I found a deposition from Max Jonas, one of the three unrelated legatees. Dr. Jonas described himself as having "a most intimate friendship" with Rotholz since their days as students at Frankfurt University, and referred to Rotholz's professional success as a foot specialist who worked in the German branch of the international firm of Dr. Scholl's Foot Appliances. He reported that Dr. Rotholz had an offer of employment from Dr. Scholl of Chicago. Things might have gone differently for Ralph Rotholz. But even though he presumably passed his licensing exam, something stopped him from taking a new position as a podiatrist in America.

Dr. Jonas testified that Rotholz had requested his assistance to get out of Germany, including help with an insurance policy to protect the valuables belonging to himself, his wife, and his sister-in-law during their travels. I stared at the words: *wife...sister-in-law.* The clock on the wall was nearing 4:45. I prayed for time to slow down.

In these dusty, discolored legal pages, I felt my mother's past come to life. Here in the depositions, I saw a marriage born of desperation, and a mature man, practiced in making legal arrangements, with connections that aided the escape from Nazi Germany. I had an impulse to thank Rotholz for helping Alice and Erika, though it didn't work out for him. His life was beginning to matter to me, and I wanted to know more than just the fate of the trunks. At that moment, turning a page, I found a startling revelation:

> In order to expatriate his capital from Germany, Testator entered into an arrangement with his then wife, his then sister-in-law, and an uncle in-law,

whereby *the uncle purchased cattle for them in Germany and exported the same to Palestine, there to be sold, and again converted into funds for the three parties in interest to the extent of their interest.* This device resulted in a substantial shrinkage of the asset value of the funds given to the uncle for the purchase of the cattle. (italics added)

A dispute arose between the parties, which was the subject of arbitration in Palestine. After the Testator left Germany and before he came to this country, he and his wife were divorced. His former wife subsequently remarried.

"The cows!" I grabbed Michael so suddenly that he grimaced. "The file documents the cows that Alice's uncle bought for them to convert to cash in Palestine. But when they got there, he told Alice and Erika, and I guess Rotholz too, that their cows died!"

I saw the cows jostling each other in the bowels of a freighter bound for Palestine. I saw my mother with rings and brooches sewn into the lining of her dress, gems covered by insurance purchased by Rotholz before they left Germany and later hidden by Erika where no one would ever find them.

27

Fritzi's Tale

M s. Feniger, it's closing time. We need you to return the file now."

The voice of the clerk pulled me back to the sterile room. I managed to hand the file over to Michael to copy the pages about the cows and the listing of the legatees, including Gustav Kohlhagen and his young daughter, Fritzi. As I walked back to the desk, I desperately flipped through the remaining pages. I didn't see anything compelling but was crestfallen to have to stop. I hoped that I hadn't missed anything critical in my haste. Contrary to clichés about New Yorkers, the woman was sympathetic even at five p.m. on a Friday afternoon.

"Did you find what you were looking for?" she asked.

"Yes," I answered. "Thank you for your help."

I was excited about what we had seen and sad to leave the documents behind to rot in the courthouse basement. I vowed not to betray Rotholz's existence. Like Selma Hamburger, who died in the camps, my grandmother Nelly, who lost all hope, or Sidy Rayfeld's mother and brother, who were sent back to Warsaw, Ralph Rotholz deserved to be remembered.

Walking back to the subway, I was exhausted and cold. I stumbled on the stairs leading down to the station and bumped into a woman who was rushing to catch her train. I would have fallen if Michael hadn't caught me, his firm hand under my arm.

Monday morning, our last day in New York, Michael and I made one last attempt to find records from the court case involving the trunks. We took the subway to the Hall of Records, now called New York Surrogate's Courthouse on Chambers Street. Endless rows of 3-by-5-inch drawers contained typed or handwritten cards with names of plaintiffs or defendants. We tried every name we could think of—Lewin, Wojewoda, Wedgewood, Feniger, Kohlhagen, Rotholz, Holz—but found nothing. Disappointed, we followed the clerk's suggestion to go to the King's County Courthouse in Brooklyn. After another crowded subway ride, we found the office, sat on stools, and scanned five years of microfiche, sliding the film up and down under the projector, searching for the familiar names. But at the end of the day, we had nothing. Any lawsuit concerning the trunks seemed to have vanished. I was ready to give up.

When we returned to California, my friend Terri decided to hunt on the Internet using every name in the Rotholz file. After a few days we decided that the only person mentioned in the probate case young enough to still be alive was Fritzi Kohlhagen. We found a newspaper announcement of her marriage to Gerald Thorner in 1952, and eventually discovered a comment she had posted on a website from a cruise she and her husband had taken. There we found the lead we had been hoping for—an email address.

I wrote immediately, explained that I was distantly connected to Ralph Rotholz and wondered if Fritzi would be willing to talk with me. I didn't hear back, but following more threads, I found a Florida address and phone number for Fritzi and her husband Gerald.

I finished my Saturday morning cup of tea and picked up the phone. My heart raced as I dialed the number, and a woman's voice answered.

"Hello. Am I speaking to Fritzi Kohlhagen Thorner?" I asked.

"Yes."

"I know this might sound strange, but I am the daughter of parents who were from Leipzig, and I am trying to learn more about Ralph Rotholz."

After a very brief pause, she said, "What do you want to know?"

I filled her in some more, and soon discovered that she was a warm and open person who once loved Ralph Rotholz very much.

"He was my *Onkel* Ralph," she said. "When I was a little child in Germany, he came to our house every Sunday night, and my mother made his favorite dish—pea soup. He was a lady's man," she added, "a handsome gentleman whose house always smelled of leather."

When I asked about his marriage to Erika, Fritzi recalled her parents saying that he had had romantic relations with both Erika and her sister. Neither she nor I chose to say more about what this meant, but I remembered Willy's comment that the two girls went wild, that they shared lovers.

Fritzi was six when her parents came to Brooklyn in 1936. Her father, Gustav, was Ralph's best friend and colleague.

"Ralph had been a diplomat in Orthopedics," she explained. "That means he had already achieved a high status, and it was terrible blow for him to have to begin over. My father had planned to join him in New York and open a practice together on Park Avenue. Our arrival in New York was a shock. The minute we landed, his sister met us at the boat and told us he was dead. My father was devastated." She paused. "He never got over Ralph's death. My father felt he had let his friend down. Every year he visited the grave where Ralph was buried."

Fritzi didn't know much more about Ralph, but she had a vivid memory of someone else. "I was just a little girl, and one day a beautiful tall woman with dark hair came to see my father. She brought me a miniature glass tea set. They talked a long time about *Onkel* Ralph. I believe the woman was Erika."

The court documents indicated that Gustav had spent two months with Ralph and his wife in Ascona, Switzerland. He and Erika knew each other.

I found Gustav Kohlhagen, listed with his wife, Meta, and daughter Fritzi, in the Ancestry.com records. They arrived on the *S.S. Berengaria* on July 21, 1936. Rotholz took his life on July 13, 1936, just eight days before his friend and colleague arrived. I thought of how little even good friends know about each other's suffering, and the price we pay for missed communication.

28

The Call

We had lived in our El Cerrito home for four years and the thrill still hadn't worn off. Michael added a deck to the back and I had planted a larger vegetable garden. I continued to sift through information that might pertain to Leipzig, and in March of 2003, I got a break. I received an email from a man in Leipzig:

> *Dear Mani,*
>
> *A friend in San Francisco sent me your article in the Jewish Bulletin. Maybe I can help you find what you are looking for.*
>
> *Matthias Wiessner*
> *Universität Leipzig*
> *Institut für Kulturwissenschaften*

Who is this man? I wondered. An old Jew who miraculously survived the war in Germany? I pictured Matthias with wisps of white hair and a long beard. How odd and mysterious it was that a seed planted two and a half years ago in the article for the *Jewish Bulletin* had born fruit. A stranger from Germany had answered my call.

I saw from his email that Matthias worked at the University of Leipzig. I wrote back immediately and told him I wanted to know about Leipzig during the period my family lived there, the twenties and early thirties, and about the neighborhood where my mother grew up, the Musikviertel. I gave him my father's name as well.

Matthias turned out to be a font of information about Leipzig. He sent me articles about its history, as well as descriptions of the current city. He also looked up my father's records at the university.

> *Today I did some searches in the university archive,*
> *because you wrote that your father, Jakob Fez Feniger,*
> *studied law at the University of Leipzig. Yes he did*
> *and I found him. His inscription was 1928.*

Matthias included an attachment with my father's registration form. I noticed that I didn't have the same drive I felt to explore my mother's life; perhaps the emotional connection to my father was interrupted by his early death, while my mother's influence on me remained strong and enduring.

Matthias recommended two books: "These books have pictures of the Musikviertel where your family lived in Leipzig," he said. To my amazement, a Berkeley librarian was able to order one of these books, *Das Leipziger Musikviertel,*[14]

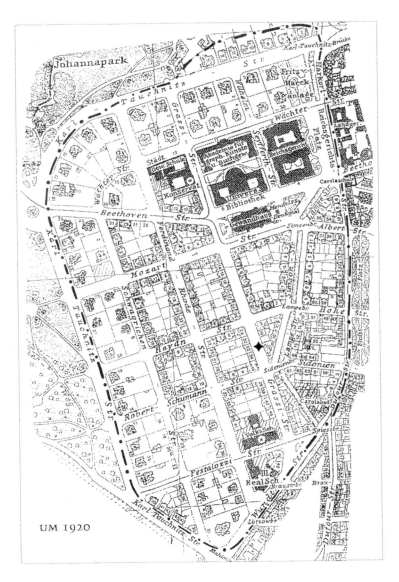

Map of the Music Quarter in Leipzig

◆

32 Grassistrasse

from a special library collection in New Jersey, for a $20 fee. When it was in my hands—an 8½" by 11" paperback, the text in German and photos on every page—I couldn't wait to open it. I just stepped to the side of the next person in line and scanned through the pages, devouring impressions of the city that had once been no more than an empty grave in my mind.

The title page had a colored aerial photo of the Music Quarter in its prewar glory. I saw an imposing Romanesque building with columns and a dome, red tiled roofs, block after block of rectangles in perfect rows, manicured landscape, a circular fountain with paths leading in four directions, two black-and-white pictures of Grassistrasse around 1910, five-story buildings of brick and cement with stone facades interrupted only by the endless repetition of window, dormers with steep roofs, cobblestone streets with trolley tracks, sparse trees with bare branches. I wondered if the street would have seemed friendlier in spring.

I returned home, ignored my growling stomach and the phone messages, and sat at the kitchen table hunched over my book. Using my Pons German-English dictionary, I tried to translate an article entitled "Meine Geliebte Ecke," (My Beloved Corner). I only got through the first paragraph. It said:

I grew up in the Musikviertel. We withstood the firestorm [*Feuersturm*] in the basement of Beethovenstrasse 23, when in February 1945 an air raid befell us [*zusammenstürzte*]. What a wonder that the lights did not go out.

But eventually the lights did go out. The fortresslike buildings that appeared so impenetrable were destroyed. Page 162 had photos from the end of the war—Haydnstrasse in 1945, the solid structures bombed and burned beyond recognition, broken walls and cavities where there once were windows, a world uninhabitable by human beings. Outside Beethovenstrasse 23, women in loose pants with scarves over their hair bent over to collect bricks and organize them into rows. They reminded me of a photograph by Henri Cartier-Bresson entitled "Dessau, Germany, 1945," an image of a woman collapsed over a pile of bricks, her face cupped in her hands. I was touched by the pathos of her posture, and aware of how much sympathy I felt for the German *Frau,* as devastated as the building that once stood on that site.

Later I studied a map of the Musikviertel dated 1920, the year Max bought the property. Six streets ran north to south, six east to west, bordered by Johannapark at the north end. I noticed blurred numbers in little squares, and all of a sudden it clicked that they were the addresses. I ran my index finger along Grassistrasse. The block between Mozart and Haydn went from 14 to 26. My finger crossed Haydn. The next block, from Haydn to Schumann had only four addresses. I counted 28, 30…32! In the center of the block on the left as I looked toward the Gewandhaus was 32 Grassistrasse. I had arrived at my mother's door.

I felt a quivering in my stomach as I trod on forbidden territory. I had to close the book and collect my thoughts. I heard the ticking of the clock; a car door slammed, the refrigerator hummed. Then I saw them, young Alice and Erika walking home from school on a cold day in November.

Against the backdrop of unyielding stone, they seemed innocent and vulnerable. I saw the cobblestone street outside their home, and the impact of Nelly's fall seemed so much harder.

I thought of Alice's past as a play made up of scenes and characters. I had a growing sense of that life from the Musikviertel book, but not quite enough to get the full flavor. I wanted concrete details: street car routes, parks, museums, theaters, restaurants. I had used Baedeker guides when I traveled in Italy, and I wondered if there was one for Leipzig in my mother's day.

My excitement was contagious, and Terri went online again. She sent queries to book dealers all over the world. Skillful and persistent, she followed every lead she found in the International League of Antiquarian Booksellers and eventually got an email from Bernard J. Shapero Rare Books, in London. Ilka Rauch wrote that the edition of interest would be *Northern Germany, Excluding the Rhineland,* Leipzig, 1925. The book collector explained that Baedeker guides were printed in Leipzig, and this was the last English edition, the only one published between the wars. The challenge was to track down a copy.

In the meantime, Mom's city was coming to life on its own. Matthias sent me a map of Leipzig printed in 1938. I unfolded it on my dining room table. This view painted a city nestled on the Weisse Elster and Pleisse rivers, with blue canals that meandered through many neighborhoods alongside broad green parks and meadows.

I looked up Grassistrasse in the index of streets, squares and bridges, and found it in FG5. Now I could position the

Musikviertel in relation to the rest of the city, a triangular section near a large expanse of green that included König Albert Park. Alice and Erika could easily have walked down Haydn Street or Mozart Street to play in the park. Was this the green, fragrant sanctuary she remembered the evening she rested in my home in Berkeley and talked about her childhood? Very likely it was, or perhaps Johanna Park just to the north.

On my birthday in 2004, Terri presented me with a small package covered with customs stamps. I looked at her in disbelief and paused to assess its size and weight. I wanted to stretch my anticipation and savor the significance of the moment. I opened the package, then carefully slid the tissue paper off a small volume, four inches by five inches, with a red leather cover and gold letters: *Baedeker's Northern Germany*. I ran my fingers over the recessed letters on the cover and turned the yellowed pages to feel their texture. The paper was thin and delicate, the print small. It had a heading for each city, with 165 folded maps interspersed.

But I wasn't interested in all the northern German cities. I skipped to the place marker, two very soft ribbons, faded red and faded blue, resting on page 213. The heading at the top of the page was "Leipzig."

This was the world where Alice grew up, the backdrop of her childhood, her youth, her coming of age. She walked to the Neues Theater, chiefly for opera, Central Theater for operettas, or with her parents to the Kristall-Palast, a variety theatre. Under Concerts it noted the Gewandhaus, every Thursday evening in winter, tickets nearly all taken by subscribers according to the guide, rehearsal Thursday morning at 10:30...Thomaskirche, motets sung by the Boys' Choir every Fri. at 6 p.m., every Sat. at 1:30. And then Art Exhibitions...Museums (many of these)...Zoological Gardens...the Palmengarten, with a restaurant and concert hall.

The train station had a sandstone façade 325 yards long, "about three football fields," Michael volunteered, and it was a hub for trains from Berlin, Breslau, Posen, Dessau, Halle, Dresden, Chemnitz, Frankfurt, and beyond. One could board a tram with a red ring on the number plate to go from the main railway station to Augustusplatz. I wondered if swans still lived in the popular square as Dr. Schmerl had described. I read about churches, hotels, restaurants, government buildings, parks, and monuments. I found a city bustling with commerce, culture, and recreation, endless venues for Alice and Erika to visit with the cousins, aunts, and uncles in the reunion photograph from 1927, to socialize with their school friends, and to rendezvous with their boyfriends.

Leipzig must have opened itself to their young and eager hearts and welcomed them to explore, only to close its doors to them with *Juden Verboten* signs. Their dreams were crushed like the brick buildings turned to rubble, in a city that by 1945 was devoid of its Jewish population.

When Tom and I had first embarked on a restitution claim for the Leipzig property, we talked about "taking the whole family to Leipzig if anything ever comes of this." By the time the settlement arrived, we both had other priorities and the thought was forgotten.

When I had spoken to Eve Wechsburg, I learned that

she and her daughter had traveled to Leipzig in 1996. The city had invited members of its original Jewish population to return and visit their former homes, stay at a hotel, eat at restaurants, attend the new Gewandhaus, and share their experiences, all as guests of the city.

Leipzig's hospitality came too late for my mother and me, but once the idea of going there entered in my mind, the magnetism of Leipzig had me in its grip. I wanted to celebrate my sixtieth birthday by making a pilgrimage to the place where my mother grew up and my grandparents had lived a significant part of their lives. I knew that this journey was no longer just to finish my mother's story. It had become mine.

Landing

As the Lufthansa wide-body airplane made its final descent into Frankfurt International Airport, I had a queasy feeling, more than the physical sensation of losing altitude. I had been squirming in a seat too cramped for my long legs for ten hours, worrying about what it would be like to be on soil with such dark history and whether I would be disappointed when I came to the end of my treasure hunt. My emotions lurched between dread and excitement as the plane taxied down the runway and came to a halt at the terminal.

"No turning back now," I said to Michael.

He lifted his hand and brushed away a few tears from my cheek.

"It's going to be fine," he said. "You've waited a long time to do this."

The idea of going to Leipzig had been brewing in my mind since Matthias first wrote me two years earlier in 2003. He sent me an electronic greeting card on every important

Jewish holiday, and I was surprised to learn that he was neither elderly nor Jewish. In his late thirties, Matthias was born and raised in Leipzig under the Socialist regime, and he was currently a doctoral student and teaching assistant at the University of Leipzig.

The moment I told Matthias that Michael and I wanted to visit Leipzig, he took the initiative and began to help me. Every few days, a new email from him would arrive.

Ok, wonderful. You are always welcome in Leipzig. Please write when you book tickets for the plane. Then I will organize a hotel for you. Hotels here in East Germany are not so expensive. I'm happy to meet you soon.

I could book a hotel in the Musikviertel, around the corner to Grassistrasse. It is a villa of a former Jewish podiatrist, built at the beginning of the twentieth century. Today it is a guesthouse of the university (not a normal hotel) and is located near all objects of interest.

Is that OK? Otherwise you can stay also in my flat and save your money for other things.

I have gotten you tickets to the Leipzig Gewandhaus Orchestra. This is where your mother and father would have gone to hear concerts. Is Friday night OK?

I arranged an appointment with the Ephraim Carlebach-Stiftung Leipzig [Ephraim Carlebach Foundation for Jewish history and culture]. Ephraim Carlebach was a famous German rabbinical family in

Leipzig. They would be happy if they could meet you and talk to you. And they would be happy if you could bring some copies of your family documents and any photographs of Leipzig.

The request for photos drew me back to the album my mother made in her youth. This time I noticed several images that hadn't caught my eye before—shots taken in the living room of 32 Grassistrasse, a picture of Alice and Erika in front of the Altes Rathaus (old town hall), and on the back of the last page of the album, a small photo of a gravesite with fresh flowers.

I stared at the last image, almost an afterthought, with no caption. I could see why I overlooked it before. All the other pages of the book evoked liveliness and passion—the laughter of schoolgirls, the joy of the ski slopes, the banter of friends and lovers. This photo was silent.

With a magnifying glass, I read the name L E W I N carved in bold capital letters across the top of the gravestone. It was harder to decipher the next row of letters but I made out Nelly on the left, Dr. Max Lewin on the right, *geboren* (born), but I couldn't read the dates of birth and death.

Again I was reminded of the twists and turns of destiny. By pure chance the photo album was in the first trunk that Uncle Curtis picked up before the family got news of the divorce. Otherwise, the photos would have been lost forever.

I wrote Matthias about the picture of the grave. He answered immediately: "If they were buried in Leipzig, we may be able to find them."

Now it was March 2005 and I was on my way to Leipzig. We could have flown to Leipzig Halle Airport, but I wanted to arrive at the main train station, the Hauptbahnhof, as my mother and father would have done. It might even have been the last place my mother saw in Leipzig when she left forever. I wanted to look out the train window at the surrounding countryside, and to feel in my body the rhythm of movement toward this auspicious destination.

Once aboard the modern, comfortable train, exhaustion took over. Michael sat opposite me so I could have a whole seat to myself. I curled my legs up and leaned my head against the cool windowpane. Eyes half closed, I watched the tall buildings of Frankfurt fade into flat agricultural land. Then the land began to swell into green hills, punctuated by the occasional dilapidated Saxon castle in the distance. I dozed off for some unknown time, then was startled awake by an unfamiliar voice.

"Mani, hello. Mani?"

I looked up at a young man with sparking blue eyes behind broad glasses. He wore a striped blue-and-white T-shirt and spoke English with a German accent. I jumped up in my seat and put my feet on the floor.

"Matthias? Is that you?"

"Yes, Mani. It is Matthias. Hello."

30

Matthias

Matthias had promised to meet us at the Leipzig Hauptbahnhof, but it turned out that he had taken the same train on his way back from a visit to his friend in Basel. He invited us to the snack car and bought me a hot chocolate and Michael a coffee. We talked until I had to admit that I couldn't keep my eyes open and needed to return to my seat for a few more hours of rest.

As the train drew near Leipzig, Matthias came to our seats again to point out the communal farming projects on the land just outside the city.

"These projects were organized under the GDR, so people from the city could have a place to grow food and the experience of working together. Each family had a small rectangular plot and a shed to keep their equipment."

I stared at this remnant of the Communist East Germany. Though it was not the original purpose of my trip, I was curious about the lives of people like Matthias, who were born under Communism and participated in the overturn of the GDR. Now that I met Matthias, I felt I could ask him questions about his own life. He said he would tell me more another day.

As the scenery became urban again, we passed several dilapidated, abandoned buildings on the outskirts of Leipzig. They were interspersed with modern or renovated commercial buildings currently in use. I was surprised that parts of Leipzig remained in a state of disrepair fifteen years after unification.

"So, we're almost there," Matthias said. "I'll meet you on the platform when we arrive."

As soon as we disembarked from the train, Matthias greeted us and took our first picture: Michael and I posed in front of the train. I am waving with a big grin on my face. I felt completely welcomed and taken care of, though I still wondered why Matthias treated us as though we were long lost family. I felt suspended between jet lag and disbelief, then realized that Matthias was asking me a question.

"Do you want to walk to Villa Tillmanns or take a streetcar?"

"I always prefer walking if it's not too far."

This was before I understood that a distance that might be ordinary for many Germans was very far for an American, even one who normally likes to walk! Dragging our rolling suitcases behind us, we followed Matthias across the lanes of streetcars, then along the Martin Luther Ring. This ring of streets that surround the center of the city reflected the site of the original town walls. Our host ran into a storefront and grabbed some traveler's maps and guide pamphlets, and then continued at a frenetic clip I soon recognized as his normal gait. Michael and I looked at each other and started laughing, two tired travelers running awkwardly after an extremely enthusiastic young man who had a concern for us that I couldn't explain.

Matthias led us down Goethestrasse, named for Auerbach's Keller, the restaurant where Faust supposedly hung out, then gestured toward the left to indicate Augustusplatz, the square I had traced with my finger on the map, where Dr. Schmerl had fed the swans and waited every Saturday to get tickets to the opera. I was sure my mother came there to hear Verdi or Mozart.

"This is a commemoration for Bamberger's Department Store," Matthias called out as he pointed to a plaque mounted on the building on the corner of Grimmaische Street. Matthias helped me translate the words into English:

IN MEMORY OF THE BAMBERGER FAMILY
WHO FORMERLY OCCUPIED THESE
BUILDINGS
AND THEIR DEPARTMENT STORE
BAMBERGER & HERTZ
THEIR LIFE WORK
THAT THE 9TH OF NOVEMBER 1938
ON KRISTALLNACHT
BY THE NATIONAL SOCIALISTS
WAS DESTROYED.

"This is where your mother came to buy her fashionable, readymade clothing."

Beneath my mental fog, his words registered. My mother was here! I was standing on a spot where she once stood.

"There is Thomaskirche," Matthias said, pointing down a lane toward a narrow church with a tall spire. "Your mother came here on Saturday afternoon to hear the Boys' Choir sing Bach motets."

I was in an altered state induced by sleeplessness and awe, but I got the eerie feeling that Matthias really knew my mother. *This is no impersonal tour of Leipzig,* I thought. *We're walking in her footsteps.*

But we were still not at Villa Tillmanns. Matthias ran into an office to obtain a key for our lodging, and then made a small detour to the Exhibition Hall of the university where his mother, Frau Brigitte Wiessner, worked. She had a warm smile but didn't speak English. I managed a few words in German: "Guten Tag, Ich bin glücklich… Good day, I am happy to meet you."

Once we crossed over from the Martin Luther Ring, we turned off Harkortstrasse onto Wächterstrasse.

"We are now in the Musikviertel, where your mother grew up," Matthias said. "A part of the university is just down the street, but it is the vacation and most classrooms and offices are closed now. Except the original main building with the university library," he pointed to the back of a building on the next block. "That is where your father studied law. We will go there tomorrow."

At last, we were standing in front of a three-story brick villa with a wrought iron gate. "Villa Tillmanns," Matthias announced. "Built in the early 1900s by a Jewish doctor.

Now it is a guesthouse owned by the university." Villa Tillmanns, Wächterstrasse 30.

I already knew the view from the Leipzig Musikviertel
book. Though the fountain itself was gone, Villa Tillmanns
was located behind the square where the fountain once
stood, the picture with paths going in four directions. I had
stepped right into the photograph from my mother's day. It
was as though the Villa had remained suspended in time,
waiting for me.

We had arrived at our destination. I took a deep breath
and turned to Matthias.

"Vielen Dank," I said to Matthias. "Thank you for your
kindness."

I hesitated, then looked directly into his eyes. "But why
are you doing this for me?" I asked.

"Because it was my loss too," he answered, and we stood
quietly together for a moment before going inside.

31

Roots

Tangled weeds, dried twigs and rocks, bare branches, and the first tufts of new spring grass protruded through the last of fall's crinkled brown leaves, marking the patch of ground that had once been number 32 Grassistrasse. I stared at the derelict property, my family's home before our roots were pulled from the ground. I wanted to dig through the dirt for a relic—the ring or broken cup that firestorm victims hold up on the evening news as a token rescued from devastation.

I leaned my weight on Michael's arm, grateful for the solidness of his support.

"I think my mother's here with us now," I said, and he nodded his head in agreement.

"I came back to find you and to understand what you left behind, Mom," I called out to the empty lot. The sun was setting, and the air became colder. Even though I wore my down coat on this last day of March, I shivered, and Michael put his arm around my shoulder.

"We'll come back tomorrow in daylight," he said. "Let's get something to eat."

I laughed in spite of the auspiciousness of the moment. I was starving. Except for our drinks on the train, we hadn't eaten since early morning. We turned and walked quietly back up Grassi toward Beethoven Street, where we found a crowded café. Candles in glass cups on each table were the only source of light. The cigarette smoke was oppressive, and it was so dark I could hardly see Michael's face across the table. But the shadows felt comforting, edges melted into each other, nothing too distinct.

I had hoped that once we were in Germany, the words would just come to me naturally, like a child who once knew a language and could pick up the familiar thread. But now, staring at the menu without my dictionary, I couldn't translate the words and the young waitress wasn't helpful. In the dim light, I recognized the word *Kartoffeln,* potatoes. Chicken and potatoes sounded great. I managed to point to chamomile tea and some coffee for Michael. An hour later we returned to Villa Tillmanns and I dropped into a restless sleep.

The next morning in the dining room of the guest house we ate a breakfast reminiscent of my mother's diet— soft-boiled eggs kept warm in little quilted bonnets, smelly cheeses, liverwurst, salami, whole grain bread, and yogurt. Matthias arrived on his bicycle and made a dramatic stop in front of us like a knight on horseback bringing his steed to a halt.

"This university building," he explained as he led us across the street, "is on the site of the nineteenth-century

Gewandhaus Orchestra Hall that was bombed during the war. It was famous throughout Europe for both music and elegance. The hall was rebuilt in Augustusplatz. The original hall is where your mother went to hear concerts. It was only a short walk from her house. I was able to get your tickets at the student rate."

I looked with awe at the tickets to the Leipzig Gewandhaus Orchestra that evening. There were two pieces on the program—Edward Elgar's Cello Concerto in E minor and Richard Strauss's *Eine Alpensinfonie* (An Alpine Symphony), conducted by the young, innovative British conductor Daniel Harding.

"I went last night with my mother," Matthias added. "The Elgar piece made me weep."

When Matthias placed the tickets in my hand, I felt that I was being handed a family tradition. I remembered my mother taking me to Carnegie Hall and the Metropolitan Opera when I was a child. I liked the excitement of the elegantly dressed women and the buzz of the audience, though I often got bored with the singing. The memorable exception was Verdi's *Aida*. The Egyptian costumes in brilliant golds, reds, and blues, and the stage sets that represented the epoch of the pharaohs, kept me in awe for the whole evening. I leaned forward from our seats in the balcony and fiddled with Mom's binoculars in an effort to study every detail. As an adult I appreciated the tradition even more and did my best to keep it alive by taking Sarah to the ballet to see *The Nutcracker* and *Romeo and Juliet*. I also remembered Grandma Alice taking Sarah to a performance by Luciano Pavarroti. Afterward my daughter said, "There were so many fur coats. It was like being at the zoo."

Matthias had a plan for the morning: the university library where my father studied, then to his office to meet several of his friends, then to lunch at the student cafeteria for sauerkraut and *Wurst*, and *Quarkkeulchen mit Apfelmus*, potato pancakes with apple sauce, one of the delicious local specialties of Saxony, made with quark, which is similar to ricotta cheese. After lunch, Matthias escorted us back to Villa Tillmanns, and the afternoon was ours.

32 Grassistrasse pulled me like a magnet. Michael and I had already talked about doing a ritual to honor my family. I gathered my photos of Alice and Erika in their youth, Max and Nelly, and more recent pictures of Uncle Willy, and Mom with her cousin Lynne. Michael and I searched a grocery store down the street for matches (*Streichholz*) and a box of votive candles.

I looked around as we walked down Grassi Street to the empty lot. We passed well-kept five-story apartment buildings that survived the bombing, with sparkling windows and potted plants on the sill. I wondered if anyone living remembered when Nelly jumped from the window.

I walked to the middle of the block and looked around for the best location for a ceremony. At first I headed towards the interior of the lot but it didn't feel right. Michael went back to the street and paced slowly back and forth.

"Here," he said to me after a few minutes. "I think this is the place."

I felt a little jolt, a catch in my breath. Yes, that spot was exactly right. I found a flat rock and created a makeshift altar with two votive candles and the photos. Though it was a calm day, Michael had to shield the flame with his palms to keep it from going out. We both knelt on the ground, listening and breathing until words came.

"May all be forgiven. May everyone be liberated from any burden of blame. May the pain between my mother and her family be put to rest, no more hatred to be carried from this day forth. May the trauma between German and Jew be acknowledged and brought to completion. From this day forward, no victim, no oppressor. May all beings be free of suffering. May this land be free to nourish new life."

Michael's presence filled me with courage. I could not have gone there without him. He knew my mother and he loved her; he was the witness and companion that made this experience real, a shared memory that I could refer to in the years ahead and he would understand.

I wanted to stay longer, but there was nothing else we could think of to do. We were kneeling on the edge of an empty lot with spotty grass, naked trees, and some rubbish. A woman walked by with a large brown poodle and didn't turn her head. I gathered up our photos, but left the modest altar with its votive candles burned down to the foil holders.

"It's getting late," Michael repeated. "We've got to rest a little and then get ready for the concert. We still need to eat something before we go."

I was having trouble adjusting to the nine-hour time difference. By the time we found some soup and headed for Augustusplatz, it was close to eight.

Michael walked at a fast clip as I tried to keep pace.

The Gewandhaus had seemed so close on my little map, practically in my mother's backyard, but I soon realized that the new concert hall in Augustusplatz was halfway to the train station. By the time we reached the Gewandhaus, we were covered in sweat. It was exactly eight o'clock when we entered the door.

In the empty lobby, we were confronted by an official of the concert hall. Standing firm and unsmiling, she told us, in German of course, that the concert had begun and we could not enter.

This was impossible. I wanted to cry. This was my birthright, to go where my mother came to hear Schumann, Schubert, Mozart, and Mendelssohn. This was where her passion for classical music was born. Adrenaline flooded my brain and suddenly German words poured from my mouth.

"Es tut mir leid," I said. (I am so sorry.) "Meine Mutter war in Leipzig geboren," I explained that we had traveled so far to find my mother's world, and how much this meant to me. I begged her help: "Helfen Sie mir bitte."

Her expression immediately softened and she nodded to us to follow. She led us to the top floor and introduced us to the usher positioned there. She explained that at eight o'clock sharp (Punkt!), the doors are locked so that there can be no interruption. However, after the first movement, there is a few seconds' pause. In that brief interlude, the usher will unlock the door and allow us to enter. Just to the left of the door, we will find two seats attached to the wall where we are to sit until the intermission, when we can find our own seats.

"Danke, danke, vielen Dank," I said bowing my head to

her, as Michael and I sat down breathless, poised to spring at the assigned moment. When the pause arrived, the usher unlocked the door, and we made a mad dash before our window of opportunity closed again.

The cellist was extraordinary, his body and his cello moving as one emotional note followed the next. The performance moved me to tears as it had Matthias.

Afterward, we strolled to the Baroque fountain in the center of Augustusplatz. Just as I dug out my camera, Matthias appeared on his bicycle, coming to his characteristic abrupt halt in front of us.

"How was the concert? Here, give me the camera and I'll take your picture in front of the Gewandhaus."

I didn't ask how he knew where to find us. He took our picture and invited us out for cocoa. On the way, we made a detour to Gottschedstrasse, to the site of the Great Synagogue that was destroyed on Kristallnacht. Against the dark backdrop of evening, I saw a platform with 140 polished bronze chairs to commemorate the synagogue and the people who would never return to fill those seats.

Unlike my anti-religious mother, my father came from an Orthodox family. My paternal grandfather, Opa, Uncle Nathan, and Fez had sat here, wearing their *yarmulkas* (skull caps) and *talis* (prayer shawls) to services on Friday night. At appropriate moments, they would have stood up, holding their prayer books and nodding their heads as they recited Hebrew verses. Their faith and their respect for the Jewish religion was part of their gift to me. I vowed I would go to the synagogue when I returned home and honor them, honor my ancestors on Yom Kippur. Matthias directed me to stand next to the stone marker carved with the word "GEDENKT" (Remember). I had heard the word before in the title of the Gedenkbuch, where I had found Aunt Selma's name. The next line said, "VERGESST ES NICHT" (Forget it not). Matthias snapped the photo. Neither he nor I would forget.

32

Stronger Than Death

On Saturday Matthias took us to hear Bach motets sung by the boys' choir of Thomaskirche. He explained that these sacred choral pieces had been performed in the church twice a week long before the eighteenth century, when J. S. Bach, who is buried in the sanctuary, was the music director.

On Sunday, Matthias organized a brunch to celebrate both our birthdays even though mine wasn't until the following week. It was also a chance for us to meet his friends. He saved the search for my grandparents' graves for our last full day in Leipzig.

Monday was a beautiful day. The skies were clear and it felt like spring. We boarded a streetcar to go to Löhr Street for a meeting Matthias had arranged with the Carlebach Foundation, an organization established in 1992 to research and preserve the history of the Jews of Leipzig.

A staffperson named Heike, a serious woman with dark hair and glasses, greeted us and gave me a 1933 directory of the Jewish population of Leipzig. I was fascinated by the ads for shops: "Kleider, Mäntel, Pelse, Hüte: Hervorragendste Modelle und Qualitäten...aber Preise, wie sie heute sein müssen!" Matthias helped me translate: "Dresses, coats, fur, hats: Excellent style and quality...priced as they must be today!" I saw ads for jewelers, tailors, furniture stores, apothecaries, photo shops, even a detective, reminders of the prosperity once enjoyed by Leipzig's Jewish middle class. Among the twelve thousand Jews living in the city at that time, I found one uncle, Nathan Feniger, at Elsässerstrasse 5, and the other under his original name, Wladislaus Wojewoda, at Reissstrasse 77. There was no listing for Max Lewin, his existence already purged from the records.

We then met with another woman, who spoke mostly Russian, in the next-door office of the Jewish Community. In a crude blend of Russian, German, and English, we explained our mission and showed her the small photo of the gravestone with LEWIN engraved across the top. Leipzig had an old cemetery that was used until the early 1930s and a "new" cemetery that opened in 1928. Since my grandfather died in 1932 he might have been buried in either one.

I hovered over her desk as she fingered through papers and cards. My nerves were beginning to fray. Matthias encouraged the woman to keep looking; she responded in broken Russian-German. I retreated across the small room to take a few deep breaths as I prepared myself for disappointment. My mother had done a good job of erasing Max and Nelly from her life, and I didn't think I'd find them.

The woman called me back over with a wave of her hand and gave me a piece of paper.

Neuer Friedhof, Leipzig, Delitzscher Landstrasse
Lewin, geb. Moses, Nelly
Lewin, Dr. Max

"This is all we need," said Matthias, who had never doubted. "This shows us the location of their graves in the New Cemetery on Delitzscher Street. Your grandparents are in row 14, *Platz* [plot] 249."

I was speechless. I still didn't dare hope that we would find the grave I saw on the last page of my mother's photo album. We made copies of several documents and followed Matthias back out to the street. Michael and I followed along as he steered his bike along the street.

"Here's the elementary school where I studied," he told us as we passed a schoolyard. He said he enjoyed his childhood under the German Socialist regime. Sometimes goods were scarce, but his stepfather was good at procuring extras. An hour later, Matthias recommended we stop at an Italian restaurant on the next corner. I was beginning to wonder if he had forgotten the cemetery, but I was hungry and my legs appreciated the chance to rest.

After a tasty meal, we resumed walking. Matthias opened the front door of a four-story apartment building and put his bicycle inside. We ascended the clean polished stairs to his simple apartment. He showed us his family photos, pictures with his sister and from his high school days, and offered us something to drink. I brought up the cemetery again and he promised me that we were on our way and had plenty of time—"only a quick stop to bring the key to my mother." We arrived at the door of Frau Brigitte's apartment house, and took the elevator to her apartment. She smiled and offered me her hand, then gestured toward a pot of tea brewing in her small kitchen. I appreciated how kind it was for her to invite us into her home and did my best to calm my impatience while I drank my *Pfefferminz,* peppermint tea.

Matthias had been focused on my agenda for the last four days and now, on our final day, he wished to share some of his own life. But the sun was getting lower and I was terrified that the possibility of finding my grandparents' grave would slip away.

Finally, we boarded a streetcar for the last mile to the cemetery. It was almost four in the afternoon. We walked a block and stopped at a gate. Within was a small building with two dark red doors under a star of David. Above the door words were inscribed in bold capital letters

STÄRKER ALS DER TOD IST DIE LIEBE

Stronger than death is love. I had not anticipated the words, nor envisioned a sanctuary with carefully manicured grounds, graceful willows, deep green cypress trees bordering the walking path, ash and birch trees still bare but on the verge of bursting into a leafy canopy.

Many German cities did not preserve their Jewish cemeteries. An acquaintance had told me the sad tale of taking her elderly father back to Germany to visit his parents' graves at a cemetery in southern Germany near the French border. The front area designated for pure Germans was

well-maintained, while the Jewish section in the rear was
a neglected tangle of overgrown weeds and vines. In Germany, there are no Jewish descendants to care for the graves
of their ancestors. My friend's father stumbled amidst the
fallen gravestones but never found his parents. They left
wishing they had never come.

Leipzig was different. The city made a commitment to
respect its Jewish population and their ancestors. We met
the caretaker, a Russian Jewish immigrant who tended the
cemetery. We showed him our photo and the records we had
obtained from the Carlebach Foundation. He motioned
for us to follow him. He paced up and down several rows,
then back again. He shook his head from side to side and
shrugged his shoulders. There was a problem. Many of the
gravestones were knocked over by the Nazis on Kristallnacht
or damaged during the war. They were replaced as accurately
as possible, but some did not survive.

I was so close. I walked carefully up the lanes between
graves, breathing low and deep. I had returned to find my
family bones...stronger than death. I tried to push back my
looming sense of disappointment.

Suddenly, Matthias called my name. "Mani, here, come
here," he shouted. "We found it!"

The grave was exactly where it was supposed to be, but
we had overlooked it several times because we were trying
to match the picture. Instead of a dark polished marker
with sharp engraved letters, we stood before a weathered
stone, streaked with gray, worn almost smooth. Upon closer
inspection, the letters became discernible—LEWIN, written
across the top. I ran my fingers over the letters and shallow

cracks that once spelled Nelly and Max and their dates of birth and death. I pressed my palms against the rough stone, still warm from the afternoon sun.

Matthias walked away and left Michael and me alone. We sat close to each other, cross-legged on the grass. I reached into my pocket and took out a rose quartz stone I had brought with me from home and placed it on this grave that had remained without a visitor for seventy years, probably since my mother left Germany in 1935.

Michael and I closed our eyes, each with our own prayer. Then I spoke.

"I am sitting on the bones of my grandparents. They have crossed over to another plane and the things they did or did not do, the words they said or did not say, are no longer relevant. They are my grandparents and I thank them for the gift of life they gave to Alice, and she in turn, passed on to me. I acknowledge the pain that they may have inflicted, and forgive them for any way they caused my mother to suffer. Now Alice is also free. Like her mirage floating above the bed in Roosevelt Hospital, she has returned to her pure spirit."

I turned to Michael. "The family legacy of loss and pain stops here, stops with me." I said. "It's not the legacy I'll pass on to Sarah. I offer her instead a story of understanding and respect, with this precious link to her grandmother Alice, and her great grandparents Nelly and Max Lewin. I pray that they may all stand behind her now, and give her a strong foundation to go forward in her life to pursue her own dreams."

Michael reached out and took my hand and said, "Amen."

33

Crossing the Border

The train was pulling out of the Hauptbanhof. We had arrived there just six days earlier, yet I felt that my whole life had shifted since then and I was on the verge of a new beginning, unencumbered by the secrets of my family's past. I had learned some disturbing things over my fifteen-year search, but I was no longer haunted by the sense that there was some missing piece I needed to know to make sense of my own life. I leaned my head against Michael's shoulder, lulled into reverie by the steady vibration of the moving train.

We were on our way to the Czech Republic to spend the last few days of our trip in Prague. I was sad to leave Leipzig, and certain I would come back again someday. I saw the city as a catalyst for my own rebirth—a focal point where past and present came together and the harsher events of my mother's history were eclipsed by my firsthand experience and the welcome we received from Matthias, his mother, and his friends. Though I knew loss and my own share of adversity, I had so much more evidence to trust life in a way my mother did not. I had found the peace of mind I was seeking.

I recognized the woman in the photograph as my mother. She did what was needed to survive her time in history and the trials of her personal journey. The pictures in her album showed me that she had grown up steeped in luxury, but she learned to be frugal and pragmatic when her privileged world collapsed. Whatever trust or openness she sacrificed in the process, she made up for in determination. When my father died, there was no soft spot to land. She drew on a hard, cold shield to keep her grief from spilling out, and she learned to type and take dictation to support us. She was proud of her versatility and showed me that there was always a way to get up in the morning and do what you have to do. Later, out of necessity, she made an unhappy marriage. Eventually, she left the husband but kept her hard-won foothold in Manhattan.

When I visited Leipzig, I realized that her Manhattan neighborhood was a perfect mirror of the Musikviertel of her youth. Instead of the Gewandhaus, she had Lincoln Center with the symphony and the opera. In the place of König Albert Park, she had Central Park to stroll through and inhale the greenery she remembered from earliest childhood. She came full circle, returning to a lifestyle that suited her, resurrected in a one-bedroom penthouse on Central Park West.

I also understood more clearly than before that I was not my mother, that the circumstances of my life offered me very different choices. I appreciated many things she gave me—her practicality, her spirit of adventure, her passion for

classical music, her courage to face new situations, prepared
or not. I always knew she loved me, but I didn't need to accept everything she gave me, like her fears that people would
let you down when you needed them, or the conviction that
danger lurked behind every unguarded moment. This part
of my inheritance I gently buried in the Leipzig cemetery. I
was reminded of it though, by an incident that occurred just
before we crossed the Czech border.

In Dresden, the last city on the German side of the border, we got off the German car and boarded the train that
would carry us to Prague. The Czech train was dark and old
compared to the modern German railroad. The conductor
indicated with his gestures that there were no assigned places
and we were free to sit anywhere. We found an empty compartment with seats upholstered in worn red velvet, with
scarred wood paneling the walls and framing the windows.
The acrid smell of cigarette smoke clung to everything.

It was an overcast day. I stared through the dirty windows at the River Elbe that ran along the tracks. Then, just
before we reached the German-Czech border, three men in
police uniforms pushed open the sliding door of our compartment and stepped inside. The tallest one, an unsmiling
man in knee-high leather boots, a khaki uniform, and short-
brimmed cap, barked "passports" at us, thrusting his hand
out authoritatively. His uniform, his manner, and his tone
frightened me, and my heart started to pound.

My anxiety was exacerbated by the fact that our passports
had not been stamped when we landed in Frankfurt. For
reasons unknown to me, the young agent had only glanced
at our names and waved us through the gate. Suddenly, that

omission seemed serious. The officer took our passports and motioned to his two partners to follow him. I could hardly breathe. Was it possible that we would be arrested, detained, or even incarcerated? It was as though time collapsed, and I became Alice clinging to her sister Erika as they embarked on an unknown destiny. I forgot that I was an American citizen living in 2005.

Moments later the guard returned followed by his cohorts. In a loud and aggressive tone, he asked why our passports weren't stamped. I told him as well as I could in my remedial German what happened in Frankfurt. I felt the sweat on my forehead and my heart pounded even faster. He shrugged his shoulders, muttered to his comrades, "Ach, Frankfurt," and handed us back our passports. Without a word to us, he turned on his heel and walked away.

For the next few minutes I sat trembling as Michael put his arm around me and pulled me closer to him on the seat. Elated by our time in Leipzig, I had forgotten that I must also accept the darker forces of history that had shaped my mother's life. I remembered the words of Winston Churchill: "Those that fail to learn from history are doomed to repeat it."[15]

Slowly, I calmed down. I sighed with gratitude that I had been given the life I had, though my heart still ached for two young women thrust into a hostile world seventy years ago. When I looked out the window again, the words on the signs and buildings were impossible to decipher. We had crossed the border into the Czech Republic.

We rose early the next morning, the actual day of my sixtieth birthday, and took the tram to the Staromestska stop. We walked to the Old Town Square in the center of the Prague, and I stood under the six-hundred-year-old Astronomical Clock, threw my arms into the air, and spun around in a circle. I felt the ground under my feet, my legs supported by the ancestral bones that connected me to the past, and my hands open to the mysteries of the future.

Epilogue

Several months after my return from Leipzig, I had a dream about my mother.

I am walking into a familiar house, perhaps my childhood home, and across the room I see my mother sitting on the couch. She appears as I remember her from our last visit, a halo of gray in her hair, a sparkle in her eyes, smiling with apple-red lipstick. I had so often imagined how much I would give just to have an afternoon with her and I want to go right to her, but there is an obstacle blocking the door.

I easily move some heavy cabinet out of my way and run to her. I can't believe she's here with me and I can finally find out everything I've wanted to know.

I take out the photo of the two sisters. "Now I can ask you all the things I've wondered about for so long," I say.

She stands up and comes toward me. I am overwhelmed with love for her. "Why would I spend this precious time asking you questions?" I whisper in her ear. We fall into each other's arms.

I woke up with tears of joy still in my eyes.

Afterword

This is not the end of the story. Once the door to my mother's past had been opened, new discoveries and insights continued to surface. A stranger from Canada, who was searching for his own lost family with the surname Lewin, found a medical book on employing the jacket crown, written by "my dentist grandfather." He generously sent me a worn green volume filled with instructions and diagrams, published in Leipzig in 1925.

I often put roses in the fluted silver vase that had once belonged to my mother. One day, using a magnifying glass to study a photo in her album, I recognized the same vase. This very item had once stood on the mantle in the living room of her home at 32 Grassistrasse.

Taking out the set of family silver Tom had sent me, and carefully polishing each piece with a soft cloth, I felt the weight of the knives and forks in my hand, each engraved with the family crest of the letter *L* for Lewin, intertwined with *M* and *N*. I realized that they must have a wedding present for Max and Nelly. Both the vase and silver would have been packed in one of the trunks that Alice and Erika sent to New York. I decided to use the silverware for special occasions, savoring the taste of connection with my relatives in the 1927 Leipzig family reunion photo.

On October 6, 2006, I received a letter from the Holocaust Victim Assets Litigation Committee:

> The Claims Resolution Tribunal is pleased to inform
> you that your claim(s) and the claim(s) of the fam-
> ily members you represent are eligible for a Plau-
> sible Undocumented Award in the amount of US
> $5,000.00 each. Your award has been approved by
> the Honorable Edward R. Korman, the presiding
> judge in the Holocaust Victim Assets Litigation.
>
> The Court has recognized that of the approximately
> 6.8 million accounts that were open or opened be-
> tween 1933 and 1945, the subsequent destruction
> of documents by the Swiss banks has eliminated
> the records for nearly 2.7 million accounts. As the
> Volker Committee recognized in its December 6,
> 1999 Report on its audit of Swiss banks, this de-
> struction of records has created an "unfillable gap"
> that can now never be known or analyzed for their
> relationship to victims of Nazi Persecution.

I was grateful to receive this acknowledgment, and I
understood the meaning of "unfillable gap." They were
offering a settlement in return for my agreement to file
no future petitions. At least they didn't say that my cows
had died.

The person I most wanted to tell about this was Lynne,
though I didn't know if she would be able to take my call.
I had last seen Lynne in May 2006, when Michael and I

were in New York. She invited us for dinner at Centolire on Madison and 86th Street. When we met in the lobby, she reached out her arms with her characteristic warm smile and sparkling eyes. She wore a bright red tailored suit and a gray silk scarf artfully secured at her neck with a dazzling brooch. Though she was eighty-five years old and leaned heavily on a shiny black cane, she was still Lynne. The waiters all knew her, and she needed only to wave her hand or give a slight nod of her head for them to rush over to the table and provide whatever she wanted.

"She's a very gracious woman," the maitre d' told me as we were leaving.

But by October, Lynne was very ill with lung cancer. I dialed her home and got her daughter Diane.

"There is no further treatment," Diane said straightforwardly. "The people from hospice care are here and they've been wonderful."

I felt awkward calling to tell her about the Swiss bank award, but Diane, whom I had never met, assured me that she heard the story from her mother many times.

"Our mother would want to know," she said. "I'll talk to her when she wakes up."

A few days later, Diane called to tell me that Lynne was eating more and felt ready to talk. A moment later I heard Lynne's voice on the phone, weak but clear.

"How are you and that sweet man of yours?" she said in her familiar way.

I told her we were fine and so glad that she and I had had gotten to be so close over the last years.

"The coin goes both ways," she answered.

I asked if her daughter had told her about the "plausible" Swiss bank account.

"Yes. I'm so happy that you and your brother will be getting something. In the scheme of things, it isn't a tall tree," she added, "but it means something."

"It means a lot," I agreed. "You know, Lynne, your words, all you've told me will live on. You've given me such a beautiful gift. I love you."

"I love you too," she said after a pause. "I'll think of more things to tell you the next time we talk."

Lynne passed away peacefully at her home on November 26, 2006. She was beautifully dressed in a silk bed jacket, surrounded by her loved ones.

I had discovered so much more than I expected. As I sat over my computer sorting out the details, sometimes laughing at the absurdities, sometimes weeping for the poignancy of the story, I missed my mother more than ever, but it was a sweet, healing grief I had never known before.

In 2009, Sarah and her fiancé Brett were married in a garden ceremony in the Santa Ynez Mountains overlooking Santa Barbara. I wore the diamond ring Alice designed when she was sixteen years old. It rained lightly that June morning, but by the time Sarah and Brett said their vows under the flowing white silk canopy, the sky was brilliant blue with only a few remaining wispy clouds. I held my hand with the sparkling ring up to the light as my mother had once done, and knew she was there smiling.

Poems from Alice's Notebook

To Erika
November 9, 1982

Your age now reached another round number
To me you are still a green young cucumber
But when hit by wanderlust's dreams of exotic nights
Please make sure next time to pick a place without parasites
Needless to say my love for you will never fail
But all I can do is expedite my wishes by mail
From *Soeurchen* to *Soeurchen* kisses, health and all the best
I drink a Schnaps to a super Geburtstagfest.

To Bill (Willy)
December 14, 1982

Camus said aging means going from passion to compassion
Bill, for your birthday, here comes my confession
With time you mellowed like a fromage de Brie
And lately your disposition even softened towards me
Try hard to make your birthday real sunny
I send you blasts of good wishes
May your future be a real honey.

To Tommy
August 14, 1979

I can't believe you're already 42
Being self-conscious and vain I know this is true
Since birthday cards were never my style
Accept these wishes with a smile
Now that you're a man of a certain age
To figure out a real gift for you one must be a sage
Let's plan for future tickets for the Met
You might prefer this to shirts, shorts or a hat
Happy birthday, all the best, my dear Tom
Let's celebrate this for many years with your old Mom.

To Terry-Mani
April 8, 1986

To make a poem for someone age 40 takes little brains
But to rhyme with 41 requires real pains
If wishes work, the super best to you
May all your hopes and wishes always come true
See you soon and admire your charm and grace
And we'll take loads of time to gossip and embrace.

Acknowledgments

No one creates a book alone. During the twenty years of my journey, many wonderful people came forward to help. This book is a testament to community, collaboration, and faith. It is also a reminder to make time to be with the people who matter to us; as I write these acknowledgments, I am saddened to note that so many of the individuals who contributed are no longer here.

Thank you to the editors who worked on different versions of the manuscript: Elianne Obadia for her insights on the first draft, Allen Horne for his attention to rhythm, Ann Matranga for giving the story roots, Rebecca Spence for pulling the threads together, and Leslie Tilly for her review of every detail. My gratitude forever goes to Naomi Lucks for championing the book from the first moment she read the manuscript, over a decade ago, to the last word. With patience, humor, and endurance, Naomi has contributed the brilliance of her writing, editing, and insight.

I appreciate the late Max Osen for his work with restitution, David Roland for legal assistance, Jim Mahoney at the Nyack Historical Society, and the Ephraim Carlebach Foundation for preserving the history of the Jews of Leipzig.

I am grateful to Carol Ehrlich for her cover vision, Patricia Coltrin for her dedication and passion for type, Karin Kinsey for artistic teamwork, Romy Harness for the author photo, and Raphael Shevelev for bringing the photographs of Alice and Erika back to life.

I want to express my appreciation to Loie Rosenkrantz for her reflections on the essence of the book, Ellen Friedman for her sensitive observations, Diane Mintz for her clarity, Jane Ehrlich for encouraging me to push the edges, Rosemarie and Martin Delson for their help with German, Joel Friedlander and the Bay Area Independent Publishers Association for guidance, and Selene Kramer, Mano Alexandra and Landes Good for cheering me on year after year.

My search would have ended very differently without the thoughtfulness of Gerald Rosenstein, who sent my email address to Matthias Wiessner in Leipzig. Matthias continues to be an amazing friend and guide. Thank you to Eve Wechsberg, Lynn Fogel, Fritzi Thorner, the late Sidy Rayfeld and the late Dr. Fritz Schmerl for sharing their stories with me. I am grateful to the late Terri Webb McMillan, who left no stone unturned to track down clues to my mother's past. I hope this book will honor her spirit.

The following people gave valuable feedback and encouragement: Kathy Allen, Tom Atkins, Sue Bender, Iris Bieri, Byron Brown, Chick Callenbach, Josephine Coatsworth, Denver Coleman, Theresa Tollini-Coleman, Mary Cuneo, Kathleen Curtin, Carol Dembling, Marcia Dickman, Carla Dole, Susan Feiga, Lara Forest, Sarah Jane Freymann, Liz Froneberger, Nancy Gallagher, Nancy Gardner, Brenda Garner, Rachel Gila, Jill Goodfriend, Nina Greeley, Elizabeth Gutfeldt, Caitlin Hoffman, Georgia Hughes, Kathy Indermill, Carol Johnson, Erika Kramer, Christine

Leefeldt, the late Lolli Levine, Dina Lisha, Jonathan Marsh, Merry and Terry Michaels, Claudia Miller, Naresh, Zoe Newman, Jackie Newlove, Deborah Nicholas, Linda Oppen, Susan Penzner, Willa Reister, Diane Rose, Karine Schomer, Jan Shapiro, the late Izzy and Edith Sher, Julie Silber, Laura Sobel, Nancy Tompkins, Margaret Trost, Loretta Valentine, Maliko Wallach and Martha Winneker.

I am grateful to my brother, Tom Feniger, for talking with me about our childhood. I cherish my relationship with him and with his wife, Harriet Feniger, whom I have known since she was fourteen and I was eight. A poignant thank you to my late cousins Tamara Rutman and Nao Freeman who spoke with me in the early years of my quest, to my cousin Nikki Gustafson with whom I have grown closer because of our shared love for Alice and Erika, and to my late uncle William Wedgewood, who contributed all he could. I will always treasure my relationship with the late Lynne Gordon for making my mother's story come alive and for being my ally in the search for truth.

I am blessed by my immediate family—Sarah Berger Habermann and Brett Habermann who make my heart burst with joy, and to my husband, Michael Gardner, whose loving companionship and infinite kindness have made this book possible. He read a thousand versions of the manuscript and was moved to tears every time. Our relationship is living proof that generational patterns do change, that life can bring more than you ever expected, and that it's my turn to make dinner for the next ten years.

Sources

1. Daniel Eisenberg, "Taking Down the Wall," Time, March 31, 2003 (http://www. time.com/time/specials/packages/artcle/0,28804,1977881_1977895_1978711,00.html).

2. Monika Gibas, Cornelia Briel, Petra Knöller, Steffan Held; translated by Cynthia Dyre Moellenhoff, 'Aryanization' in Leipzig. Driven Out. Robbed. Murdered, Leipzig, Germany: Leipzig City History Museum, 2009 (http://www.juedischesleipzig.de/arisierung_engl09.pdf).

3. Mary Lowenstein Felstiner, To Paint her Life: Charlotte Salomon in the Nazi Era (New York: HarperCollins, 1994).

4. Much later, I found a website with names from all of Germany: www.bundesarchiv.de/gedenkbuch.

5. Peter Gumbel, "Secret Legacies: Heirs of Nazis' Victims Challenge Swiss Banks Over Deposits from World War II Era," Wall Street Journal: June 21, 1995.

6. Henry Burstyner, "Holocaust Survivors Claims Against Swiss Banks: What's Really Going On," (no date; http://www.dosinc.org.au/swissbanks2.html).

7. Edmund L. Andrews, "The Rescuer of Swiss Bank Ledgers," New York Times, January 17, 1997.

8. David E. Sanger, "Swiss Find More Bank Accounts From the War, and Publish List," New York Times, July 23, 1997.

9. Judith Scherr, "Grandfather's Swiss Bank Account Opens Past for Berkeley Woman," Contra Costa Times, July 31, 1997.

10. Leslie Katz , "Area Jews Join Frustrating Hunt for Names on Swiss List," Jewish Bulletin, August 27, 1997.

11. Andy Altman-Ohr, "Therapist Uncovers Family Secrets, Finds Shoah Tragedy," Jewish Bulletin, October 18, 2000.

12. This was my uncle Willy's surname before it was anglicized to Wedgewood.

13. "Exiled Physician Ends His Life Here," New York Times, July 13, 1936.

14. Anne Schönfelder and Wieland Zumpe, Das Leipziger Musikviertel, Leipzig: Wiss.-Zentrum, 1996.

15. Churchill was paraphrasing George Santayana in The Life of Reason: "Those who cannot remember the past are condemned to repeat it."

Mani Feniger is available for consultation, seminars and presentations. More information may be found at her website www.manifeniger.com.

She can also be contacted at
manifeniger@gmail.com

KeyStroke Books
3060 El Cerrito Plaza, Ste. 372
El Cerrito, CA 94530

CPSIA information can be obtained at www.ICGtesting.com
Printed in the USA
BVOW05s2324271114

377003BV00001B/25/P